"I know not with what weapons World War III will be fought, but World War IV will be fought with sticks and stones."
—Albert Einstein, 1949

VOTING IN SANITY
– An Overview –

Disgusted with POLARIZED POLITICS?

What if someone told you that THE ENTIRE FREE WORLD'S VOTING METHODS ARE ALL TOTALLY DYSFUNCTIONAL and do nothing more than promote polarization and conflict at the expense of the common-ground consensus? Would you claim, "How could this be, we've had democracies here in the free world for over 200 years, and they're all working just fine (aren't they?)."

But what if we could prove it to you in under a minute? Actually, we'll do even better: we'll let *you* prove it to <u>yourself</u>—*right now*—in less than 60 seconds! Just answer this one little question:

> Suppose you're driving a small school bus with 10 hungry young hockey players coming home after a morning game, and they're all desperate to stop for a quick lunch together. <u>You</u> have to choose the <u>one</u> best place to take them. There are only two choices—a BBQ pork stand, or a pizza shop.
>
> You ask the 10 kids for their opinions on each of their two choices, and you quickly find out the following:
> - 6 of the 10 kids prefer BBQ pork over pizza
> - The other 4 kids *HATE* BBQ pork, and it's even against their religions
> - *ALL* the kids, however, like pizza
>
> Where are <u>YOU</u> going to take them: BBQ pork or pizza?...

? ? ?

...So, did you go for the please-all pizza as all *people* do? But here's the incredible problem: If this simple little two-choice selection had been put to a vote with the kids on the bus like we do in any of the free world's democracies—*all* of which restrict voters to just their single-choice 'preference' (or a set of *ranked* 'preferences'), then the polarizing pork, preferred by 6 out of the 10 kids, would have been selected by "majority rule" at 60%. But you know darn well that if you pull your bus into the polarizing pork, there's going to be a 'CIVIL WAR' on your bus when 40% of the kids will be damned to go hungry! And so, if all *people* choose one option in a simple little selection between just two choices, but all the free world's voting methods select the *other* option— *the polarizing alternative*(!), then *We the PEOPLE* can only conclude that ==THE ENTIRE FREE WORLD'S VOTING METHODS ARE ALL COMPLETELY BOGUS!==

Would you like to learn more about this voting 'insanity'? Have you ever wondered…

- Why in the United Sates do we have a two-party system—each party trying to undermine the other? (And how did George Washington first warn us against this?)

- Is it possible that ***the entire free world's voting methods are all completely dysfunctional***? (You already know the answer.)

- What precisely is *"The Will of The People,"* and how is it that no democracy is able to find it? (But *Voting In Sanity* will show you how adding just two more words to our simplest ballot instructions *will* find the common-ground consensus.)

- Is there something inherently wrong with our "majority rule" legislation—where *everyone* is supposed to do what just the 'majority' prefers? (Yup!)

- How can efficacious social-choice methodologies maximize the utility of group potential? (Okay, so you never thought about this one, but it's the backbone of smart group decisions. We'll show you how.)

- What do Internet rating methods for reviews have to do with the best voting-method practices and theory?

- How does The Media, in conjunction with our bogus voting method, play into the hands of our most polarizing candidates? (e.g., Donald Trump)

- **How was it even possible in the 2016 U.S. presidential race that the two "most preferred" front-runners—Donald Trump and Hillary Clinton—were polling as the *"least favorable"* candidates in their own respective parties?!**

- Why do most people have so little faith in and so little respect for 'politicians' and our political process? (See the above, and the below.)

- **How did the disastrous American election of 2016 epitomize all that's wrong with our 'single choice' voting method?**

- How did the disastrous Egyptian election of 2012 epitomize all that's wrong with the free world's voting methods?

- When was America first forewarned against any trumped-up authoritarian figure promising to 'save' us from the evils of the two-party system, and was George Washington the first one to officially warn us? (Yes, he was; see page 4.)

…plus you'll learn about 'the lesser of two evils,' spoilers, the longtime misunderstanding of the "one man - one vote" principle, gerrymandering, and a bunch of other stuff that you never really thought about but which totally affect the quality of your life.

Voting In Sanity thus not only explodes the myth of "majority rule" as used in our dysfunctional voting methods, but it also lays out the simple grassroots action plan for how *We the People* can take back our government from our entrenched, self-serving, two-party duopoly through a simple, virtually-no-cost, immediate and *precise* common-sense solution that will mitigate our polarized politics and **create the democracy that *We the People* deserve!**

Voting In Sanity — are you in?

THE PROPHETIC WISDOM OF
GEORGE WASHINGTON

Washington's "Farewell Address," paragraph 22
— *1796* —

George Washington warned us against <u>our two-party system</u>—each party trying to undermine the other—

> *"The alternate domination of one faction over another, sharpened by the spirit of revenge, natural to party dissension, which in different ages and countries has perpetrated the most horrid enormities, is itself a frightful despotism.*

…but then warned us about the eventual rise of an authoritarian figure who promises to 'save' us from its "frightful despotism":

> *But this leads at length to a more formal and permanent despotism. The disorders and miseries which result gradually incline the minds of men to seek security and repose in the absolute power of an individual; and sooner or later the chief of some prevailing faction, more able or more fortunate than his competitors, turns this disposition to the purposes of his own elevation, on the ruins of public liberty."*

<u>DEDICATION</u>

To all the wonderful people around the world who have dedicated
a significant portion of their lives for a more peaceful planet,
We the People thank you from the bottom of our hearts for your deep
kindness, consideration, and humanitarian efforts towards helping to
promote a greater World Peace for us all.

Visit our website (in progress): www.VotingInSanity.org – a not-for-
profit, free, global humanitarian initiative

Contact the Author: VotingInSanity@gmail.com
(For press inquiries, please put "press inquiry" in subject line first.)

==

ISBN-13: 978-1977505668

ISBN-10: 197750566X

TABLE OF CONTENTS

    Are the Entire Free World's Voting Methods Inherently Flawed?
    Why Can't the Free World's Voting Methods Find *The Will of The People*?
    Why Can't Runoff Voting Find *The Will of The People*?
    Can Single-Choice Voting *Ever* Find *The Will of The People*?
        Prove for yourself that **The Entire Free World's Voting Methods Are All Completely Bogus.**
    Does *Anyone* Really Believe In "Majority Rule"?

    What Are the Benefits of Multi-Choice Approval Voting Over Single-Choice Voting?
    Why Can't Single-Choice "Preferences" Be Used to Find *The Will of The People*?
    How Is It that Only the "Rated-Voting" Methods Can Find *The Will of The People*?

    Why Is It That No Democracy on Earth Utilizes Any Rated-Voting Methods?
    The endemic electoral dysfunction of our single-choice/plurality voting method is even worse than anyone seems to realize.
    Who Uses Rated-Voting Methods?

    Remove The "Overvote" Rule! (thus instituting Approval Voting)
    The Best Reason of All to Institute the Value-Based, Rated-Voting Methods
    Best Definitions for the Four Most Important Concepts in the Free World

    Instituting Approval Voting

    Here's How It All Went Down
    What *We the People* Are Now Facing

INTRODUCTION

On November 8, 2016, the "least favorable" presidential candidate in polling history—Donald Trump—won the Presidency of the United States as a so-called 'populist' while the "*most favorable,*" most-generally-popular candidates in the race never made it onto our general-election ballot. The next day, thousands upon thousands of outraged, indignant people spontaneously marched in the streets of towns and cities across the nation in protest to this sociological travesty—thinking erroneously that it was the 'Electoral College' that had somehow betrayed them but little knowing of the true cause of their outrage and grief: our totally flawed 'single choice' voting method that promotes the polarizing alternatives best able to *divide* us at the expense of the common-ground consensus best able to *unite* us. *Voting In Sanity* thus explains how injustices like these have been perpetrated upon *The People*, ever since the inception of our democracy, by a self-serving, entrenched political class that enjoys the benefits of our dysfunctional duopoly, and it proposes the simple grassroots plan for what *We the People*, as individuals, can do to mitigate the polarization and conflict caused by a bogus voting method that keeps electing self-serving politicians who typically cater to a rich class of donors but only have to placate a bare 'majority' of their polarized constituency in order to get themselves elected and re-elected again and again by "majority rule" without regard for the general *Will of The People*.

Thus, *WE the PEOPLE*, as the only legitimate and true Source of all political power, and in the time-honored tradition of the Declaration of Independence, do herewith announce

The People's Declaration of Independence
from Irresponsible Representation

and *We* do solemnly Pledge to rectify these inequities and injustices in the simplest and fastest manner possible for the betterment of *Our Collective Society*, insofar as it is well understood by many in our political science community that there is a simple, common-sense, virtually-no-cost, immediate and *precise* solution—to be elucidated shortly—that can best mitigate our polarized politics and create the democracy that *We the People* deserve.

We also Pledge to help prevent these same injustices from undermining emerging democracies as well, so that they may ultimately gain the benefit of truly democratic, non-partisan, non-polarizing and *peaceful* self rule, as *We* intend to help promote herein and herewith. And to support this Declaration, with a firm reliance on our own Common Sense and humanitarian will, **We the People** mutually Pledge to each other our sacred honor to implement these most important changes to effect a greater World Peace.

Thus we begin our mission for

Voting In Sanity

But first we need to understand our

<u>VOTING 'INSANITY'</u>
– "Majority Rule" vs. *The Will of The People* –

"A long habit of not thinking a thing wrong gives it a superficial appearance of being right."

—Thomas Paine, *Common Sense* (Philadelphia, 1776)

<u>Are the Entire Free World's Voting Methods Inherently Flawed?</u>

What would you say if someone told you that the entire free world's voting methods are completely dysfunctional in that they're incapable of finding the collective *Will of The People*, and that the parliamentary procedure of "Majority Rule," as used therein, is not only fundamentally undemocratic but actually promotes polarization and conflict? I'd bet you would have said they were nuts…until you proved it to yourself in our OVERVIEW a few pages back. But if you want a full understanding of just exactly what you did to prove it to yourself and where *We the People* need to go to truly take back our government from our entrenched, self-serving two-party duopoly, then you'll need to understand some accepted definitions of common political terms, such as the definition of "**democracy**," a "**vote**," an "**election**," and have a good idea of what "***the Will of The People***" is supposed to mean.

Ready to start your journey to find *the Will of The People*?

Let's start with "**democracy**":

de·moc·ra·cy
noun \di-ˈmä-krə-sē\
: a form of government in which people choose leaders by voting
—<u>www.merriam-webster.com/dictionary/democracy</u>

- -

"With the advent of Democracy, the world will be at peace, as most people would rather live in harmony than be at war with one another."

—anonymous dreamer

- -

Unfortunately, the philosophical ideal of "democracy" (literally: *The People* rule) seems to have never been realized in any modern civilization. Instead of rule by *The People*, most democracies —as we all well know—are ruled by legislators who come from, are connected with, or cater to the rich, the powerful, and the well connected, with little regard for the general *Will of The People*. Does anyone really doubt this? (And could it be that such typical disgust with your own government is the very reason you're reading this book?)

But at least in all democracies *The People* do have an input into their governance because they *do* have 'the vote.' Of course, it didn't always start out this way. At the inception of modern democracy, here in the United States, the vote was essentially given to just white male property owners. It took many decades more for *all* white men to gain the vote, and then an even greater time for people of color and women as well.

So, now that all citizens of legal age here in the U.S. have the right to vote, what is a "vote" anyway?

Even though our Constitution does not clearly define the word "**vote**," most people assume this one basic definition:

vote
noun /vōt /
1. A formal indication of a choice [a preference] between two or more candidates or courses of action, expressed typically through a ballot or a show of hands or by voice.
—www.oxforddictionaries.com/us/definition/american_english/vote

- -

> Unfortunately, as we'll soon find out, this method of voting, used by all the free world's democracies—where the voter is restricted to selecting just one choice as his 'preference,' is the very bane of democracy itself. (We'll highlight and indicate a better, more accurate, and more socially useful definition of "vote" later.)

- -

So, we now all understand that a "**democracy**" is where people "**vote**" in an "**election**."

And you undoubtedly have a good idea of what an "**election**" is:

e·lec·tion
noun \i-ˈlek-shən\
: the act or process of choosing someone for a public office by voting
—http://www.merriam-webster.com/dictionary/election

And now, finally, we have the essential ingredients of democracy:

Democracy is where people **vote** in an **election** to express *the Will of The People*.

And so, onward to the very *purpose* of democracy itself: to find *the Will of The People*.

> ***"The will of the people…is the only legitimate foundation of any government, and to protect its free expression should be our first object."***
> **—Thomas Jefferson to Benjamin Waring, 1801**

But just what is *the Will of The People*?

- -

> *"If* the Will of The People *is what an election finds, then whatever an election finds is* the Will of The People, *isn't it?"*
> —current political mindthink of 'tacit consent'

- -

Swiss-French philosopher Jean-Jacques Rousseau (in *Discourse on the Origin of Inequality*, 1754), who is attributed with coining the term "volonté générale"—the "general will," does not describe it as the will of the majority but rather as whatever best serves the common good, whatever is truly best for the state [the societal group] as a whole, *the Will of The People*. **This is the most important misunderstanding that the free world's voting methods perpetuate: that *the Will of The People* is defined by "majority rule"—the preference of the majority— instead of the preference of the whole, collective group.** (Rousseau, However, did not specify just how this true, collective *Will of The People* could be determined.)

Here's a reputable dictionary definition for "*the Will of The People*":

the will of the people [in essence, the "general will"]
[from "Full Definition of WILL"]
[4c.]: the collective desire of a group <**the *will* of the people**>
                    —http://www.merriam-webster.com/dictionary/will

Yes—the *collective* desire of a group. But just how do we determine "the collective desire of a group"?

As we've already mentioned, Rousseau does *not* describe "general will" (i.e., *the Will of The People*) as the will of the majority but rather whatever best serves the common good *for the whole, collective group*. Rousseau and other philosophers, unfortunately, never quite figured out just how to find this collective and true *Will of The People*. But that's where *Voting In Sanity* comes in.

On the following pages, you will learn not only why the free world's voting methods are inherently flawed in that they fail to find common-ground consensus and instead only promote polarization and conflict, but you will also learn how *We the People* can add just two more words to our simplest ballot instructions so that our voting methods *do* find *the Will of The People*: the collective desire of a group.

But first, let's see exactly why the free world's voting methods are incapable of finding *the Will of The People*:

- -

— *WORLD NEWS* —
Egypt, the cradle of civilization, January, 2011:

On January 25th, 2011, the people of Egypt rose up virtually as one. After 5,000 years of monarchy and autocratic rule, they'd had enough. Spurred on by the ongoing Arab Spring that had already toppled a ruler in Tunisia, the dam of frustration over authoritarian rule finally broke. The Egyptian people wanted greater freedom and equality; virtually eighty million Egyptians were demanding to become part of a new world of peace and prosperity, equal justice and equality (at least for men), and an end to almost three decades of Hosni Mubarak's autocratic rule. In other words, they wanted open, free and fair elections—a democracy where *The People* finally rule. They took to Tahrir Square in Cairo, at times over a quarter million strong, and—as the world watched—through their dogged determination, they set in motion events that would bring down a de facto dictator. And finally, after nearly a thousand lives were lost fighting for freedom, they would all get to vote in their first free and fair post-Mubarak democratic election. For their highest office in the land, the presidency, there would be thirteen viable contenders to choose from on the electoral ballot, some of whom had broad support among the Egyptian people, and one, especially, who would consistently poll as the favorite to win the election.

The election process would essentially use the same single-choice voting method that the rest of the free world uses in order to find a single *majority winner* from a diverse group of political contenders. What could possibly go wrong? . . . .

- -

Why Can't the Free World's Voting Methods Find *The Will of The People*?

Here's a simple 'voting' dilemma for you to consider:

You're part of a group of five friends who all want to meet in the city and go to a movie together. There are thirty movies in the area to choose from. Which movie is the best one for your group to see together? (In other words, which movie best represents the collective *Will of The People* for your little group here—the one movie that will give your group the greatest overall satisfaction?)

So, how would you propose that your group figures this out? Would you suggest that you all take a vote?

In order to take a vote to find the best movie among thirty contenders—the movie that best represents the collective desire of the group, your group of five friends is going to have to utilize a specific voting method. So, what do you do, draw up a ballot with the 30 movies and use the free world's single-choice voting method and ask each friend to indicate just his single favorite movie selection—his 'preference'—and then see which movie was selected on the most ballots? Think about this for a moment....

Did you conclude there's a good chance here that *none* of the thirty movies will receive more than one vote, let alone a "majority" (more than half) of the votes from the five voters? How would a single-choice, five-way tie be broken? And what if three of the movies receive one vote each while another movie receives *two* votes—should *this* movie become the "plurality winner" by simply having the most votes even though it hasn't passed some 'majority' threshold? And what if *two* movies get two votes each; should there be a runoff of these top-two vote-getters to find the so-called "majority winner"? And, lastly, even in the unlikely event that a single movie was preferred by *three* of the five voters and was thus considered the outright "majority winner," what if the other two voters would absolutely *hate* going to see this particular movie (e.g.: too scary, too sexy, too childish, etc.)?

On the other hand, what if there were an all-around good movie that your collective group would be happiest with, even if it wasn't *anyone's* particular preference? What voting method would select *this* movie?

- -
DID YOU KNOW that there are many different voting methods—different mathematical processes for choosing winners—and that each one can select a different winner from the very same set of options? (for a good, comprehensive breakdown of various voting methods, see => https://en.wikipedia.org/wiki/Voting_system)
- -

So, if the free world's 'single choice' voting method (of having each voter indicate just his singular preference) doesn't work to find the one movie out of thirty that best represents the collective *Will of The People* for your little group of five friends here, then at what point does the free world's single-choice voting method actually work: when there are 10 voters and 20 movies? 100 voters and 10 movies? 1,000 voters and 5 movies? …How about 80 million voters and just two candidates? Does single-choice voting *ever* work to find *the Will of The People*?

- -
— WORLD NEWS —
In 2012, Egypt's population (over 80 million people) voted in their first free and fair post-Mubarak democratic election. There were 13 viable contenders on the ballot. Virtually all the professional polling—even just three days before the election— showed that the moderate-centrist Amr Moussa would most likely win the presidency, especially when he was compared head-to-head in a runoff against each of the other candidates. No candidate won a majority, and Amr Moussa came in 5th place—thus ineligible for the runoff vote. WHAT HAPPENED??
- -

Why Can't Runoff Voting Find *The Will of The People*?

Okay, so you may be thinking here that single-choice voting breaks down when trying to find a majority winner in an election with thirty candidates (e.g., your five friends trying to select their best movie out of thirty choices), and that it also breaks down in an election with as many as thirteen candidates (as happened in Egypt's first post-Mubarak election). But what if there were only a *few* candidates on the ballot—perhaps just *three* contenders? If none of just *three* candidates receives a majority, then what would be wrong with dropping the worst vote-getter and having a runoff election between just the top-two vote-getters to find the majority winner? Surely *this* would be a legitimate process to find *the Will of The People*, wouldn't it?

Let's consider a hypothetical example, then, of an election with just three candidates:

> Two impassioned, polarizing, and diametrically-opposed candidates, each trying to eke out a majority of the single-choice votes to win the highest office in the land, wind up each receiving half of all the votes (thus neither side having a clear 'majority win'). And now, each of their opposing factions threatens a civil war if the other side should win in the runoff. Meanwhile, a well-respected third candidate, nicely positioned *between* the two opposing forces, was *everyone's close 2nd choice* but got no votes at all.

> Question: Which of these three candidates is best suited to lead a collective society to peace and prosperity—one of the two polarizing demagogues, after whose election in the runoff there's going to be a Civil War, or *everyone's close 2nd choice* who got NO VOTES AT ALL?

If you answered (as everyone does) that the candidate above who is best suited to lead a collective society to peace and prosperity was the *third* candidate (who didn't get *any* votes at all), then it's time to recognize *'a most peculiar political paradox'*: The preference of a collective society (i.e., *the Will of The People*) among three or more candidates might actually *not* be ANY individual voter's single-choice, first-place "preference"!

**Can Single-Choice Voting *Ever* Find *The Will of The People?*

Hmmm…so maybe single-choice voting is meant to work best when the choice is between just *two* candidates; mathematically, then, this will *have to* give us a "majority winner"—the one with the majority of single-choice votes (assuming there's not an exact tie). And in an election with just two candidates, doesn't this single-choice "majority winner" then *have to* definitively represent *the Will of The People*?

This is precisely what was proposed in the late 1700s by the enlightened French social-choice theorist and mathematician, The Marquis de Condorcet [pronounced *condor* (like the huge vulture) *say*]. He proposed the "Condorcet method" of voting—a much vaunted voting method even to this day. In the Condorcet method, each voter *ranks* the candidates in the order of his preferences (e.g.: 1st place, 2nd place, 3rd place, etc.), and the "Condorcet winner" is the candidate whom voters prefer to each and every other candidate when compared to them one at a time, head to head (as if in a simple, two-candidate, single-choice, "majority wins" race).

But does such a Condorcet "majority winner" truly represent *the Will of The People*? To test the validity of this widely-presumed and long-held supposition, let's see if its validity holds up in a simple selection between just two choices—as if it's just a simple, two-candidate, single-choice, "majority wins" race.

Consider this simple social-choice dilemma and see if it proves to your complete satisfaction that **The Entire Free World's Voting Methods Are All Completely Bogus**. Just answer this one little question:

Suppose you're driving a small school bus with 10 hungry young hockey players coming home after a morning game, and they're all desperate to stop for a quick lunch together. <u>You</u> have to choose the <u>one</u> best place to take them. There are only two choices: up ahead is a BBQ pork stand, and just down the road is a pizza shop.

You ask the 10 kids for their opinions on each of their two choices, and you quickly find out the following:
- **6 of the 10 kids prefer BBQ pork over pizza**
- **The other 4 kids *HATE* BBQ pork, and it's even against their religions**
- ***ALL* the kids, however, like pizza**

Where are you going to take them: BBQ pork or pizza?

This bears repeating: <u>**Where are YOU going to take them?**</u>...

? ? ?

…So, did you go for the please-all pizza over the polarizing pork? If you did, then, you're not alone: We have asked this very same, precise question separately to hundreds of individuals, and **absolutely *every single <u>person</u>* selects "pizza" as *the Will of The People*** for this little group just like you did! But here's the incredible problem: **If this simple little two-choice selection were put to a vote among the kids on the bus like we do in any of the free world's democracies— *all* of which restrict voters to just a single-choice 'preference' (or a set of *ranked* 'preferences'), then the polarizing pork—preferred by 6 out of the 10 kids—would have received 60% of the single-choice/first-place 'preferences' and would have been selected as the winner by "majority rule" at 60%. But you know darn well that if you pull your bus into the polarizing pork, there's going to be a 'Civil War' on your bus when 40% of the kids will be damned to go hungry!**

And thus we—the *people*—can only conclude: **Even in a simple little selection between just two choices or candidates, the so-called "majority winner"** (the one who receives more than half the single-choice/first-place votes) **does *not* necessarily represent *the Will of The People*!**

Is it any wonder, then, why there is so much polarization and conflict in the world to this day, and *especially* why there was so much voter consternation over the calamitous U.S. presidential election of 2016?

'Democracies' the world over are using totally-flawed single-choice/<u>preference-based</u> restrictive voting methods for their elections—methods that dysfunctionally select polarizing alternatives at the expense of the best common-ground consensus for *the Will of The People*!

As we've already pointed out, it was George Washington who first had the foresight to warn us against such polarizing alternatives just after his two terms in office, when he wrote to the American People in his Farewell Address that ***"The alternate domination of one faction over another, sharpened by the spirit of revenge…is itself a frightful despotism."*** But that was way back in <u>1796</u>, and we *still* have a two-party system of government—each party trying to undermine the other! **Have *We the People* learned *nothing* over the past 200 years?**

Does *Anyone* Really Believe In "Majority Rule"?

So here's **the most important thing that you have just learned**—and have proven to *yourself* in less than 60 seconds when you chose the please-all pizza over the polarizing pork:

THE ENTIRE FREE WORLD'S VOTING METHODS—where the voter is arbitrarily restricted to indicating just a single-choice 'preference' between two or more candidates or courses of action—ARE COMPLETELY BOGUS because they are fundamentally incapable of finding the collective *Will of The People*, and, moreover, the parliamentary procedure of "Majority Rule," as used therein, does nothing more than promote polarization and conflict— the very ingredients of war!

Which is why we can say with complete certainty that when the entire free world's democracies restrict voters to just their single-choice 'preferences,' then

NO ONE
believes in
"Majority Rule"

<u>VOTING IN *SANITY*</u>
– Finding *The Will of The People* –

In the BBQ Pork vs. Pizza dilemma, how is it that you were able to come up with "pizza" as the obvious *Will of The People* for those hungry young hockey players on your bus? Did you use your common-sense morality and humanitarian intuition instead of relying on arbitrary and restrictive voting rules (e.g., single-choice voting) that were prescribed hundreds of years ago? Did you intuitively consider what was best for *the whole group* (the little collective society on your bus) instead of what was best for just the majority—especially because you instinctively realized that choosing the "majority winner" here (the BBQ pork) would seriously polarize your group and might lead to a 'civil war' on your bus? Of course you did.

Instead of just restrictively asking the kids which of the two food choices they "preferred," you— the person in charge of deciding where the group should go—sensibly asked the kids for their *opinions* on (i.e., how much they *valued*) each of their two options. You then considered which of the two options would provide the greatest satisfaction (*value*) *for the whole group* and realized that <u>only six of the ten kids</u> approve of the BBQ pork (while the other four actually *hate* it) but that <u>all *ten* kids</u> approve of the pizza!

In other words, you found out how many of the 'voters' (the kids on your bus) *approve* of each option. This simple, multi-choice voting method that you intuitively used here is called "**Approval Voting**," where voters can simply vote for as many options as they approve of, and the option with the most votes wins—literally, the option that is "most approved."

- -

<u>Point of Logic #1:</u>
It is important to note that Approval Voting is always more expressive for the voter than restrictive single-choice voting because multi-choice Approval Voting *includes* single-choice voting, but single-choice voting arbitrarily *precludes* voters from giving multiple approvals should voters wish to do so.

- -

<u>What Are the Benefits of Multi-Choice Approval Voting Over Single-Choice Voting?</u>

Multi-choice Approval Voting literally finds *the "most approved" candidate of the entire collective group* instead of just the "most preferred" candidate of the largest polarizing faction. **In an Approval Voting election, many voters will want to approve of more than one candidate** because:
- there will be many more generally popular, viable, and diverse candidates on the ballot for voters to approve of (see 2nd bullet, next paragraph),
- when a voter does not have total confidence that his preferred candidate will win, he will likely want to approve of some of the other candidates on the ballot so as to differentiate them from the candidates that he *doesn't* support,
- voters who don't have a clear favorite, in that they prefer two or more candidates equally, will have the opportunity to support [approve of] as many candidates as they wish.

Furthermore, because voters can approve of as many candidates as they like, **Approval Voting provides a level political playing field** where:
- similar candidates won't be spoiling each other's chances by taking votes from one another (the 'spoiler' effect),
- more candidates will run, because their vote-totals won't be split up among other similar candidates ("vote splitting" from the 'spoiler' effect),
- candidates will be able to run on their *own* platforms and owe their allegiance directly to *The People* without having to 'adopt' any private party's agenda (its polarized "platform") nor have to pander to any private party's leadership or its polarized partisan base in order to win its primary and then have to 'walk it back' (undo all those 'fibs' they'd told to the partisan base) in order to pick up the votes of the centrists and the independents for the general election.

Approval Voting thus not only honestly encourages many more viable contenders to run for each political office, but it also encourages the individual voter to make multiple choices so that he will at least likely help to elect one of the candidates that he (and the most other voters) approve of and not wind up with a candidate that he really doesn't like at all!

Here is a hypothetical example from *The Center for Election Science* of how a filled-in Approval Voting ballot and its voter instructions would differ from a single-choice ballot:

Vote for one or more candidates. **The candidate with the most votes wins.**	
Alexis Sandoval	●
Franklin Hartsdale	●
Daisy Dukes	○
David Green	●
Joe Shmoe	○

Moreover, instituting Approval Voting—by simply removing the "overvote" rule (the rule that all such multi-choice votes shall be discarded when voters select more candidates/options than the number to which they are restricted to by state statute)—will virtually have no added costs, and it can even save us taxpayers billions of dollars by making private party primaries unnecessary— private party primaries typically restricted only to polarized partisans and which function solely to eliminate 'spoilers' to the party's front-runner but which also wind up cutting down *The People*'s choices on their general-election ballot.

- -

Is "Approval Voting" legal ? And, if so, then what does *"One Man, One Vote"* mean?

Contrary to common misunderstanding, *"One Man, One Vote"* (also called *"One Person, One Vote"*) has nothing to do with how many choices a voter can make within a closed set of options. Instead, *"One Man, One Vote"* is concerned that "the voting power of each voter is as equal as possible to that of any other voter" (see => http://elections.uslegal.com/elections-districts-and-apportionment/). The *"One Man, One Vote"* principle derives from several 1960's U.S. Supreme Court decisions which ruled that each state's legislative districts must be approximately equal in population so that each voter in the state will have approximately equal voting power to one another in electing his district's singular representative. Rationale: Imagine that your state has only two districts. District #1 contains just one person—your arch enemy, and District #2 contains everyone else in the state, including you. Would it be fair to have a legislature composed of just the two single representatives from each of these two districts? Note: Crafty political parties have found a way to subvert the egalitarian effects of *"One Man, One Vote"* and gain greater political leverage in spite of states legally needing to have equally populated districts: "Gerrymandering" —re-drawing congressional district lines to give one political party a voting advantage over another. Here's a simple pictorial that quickly illustrates the point:

"Gerrymandering, explained – Three different ways to divide 50 people into five districts":

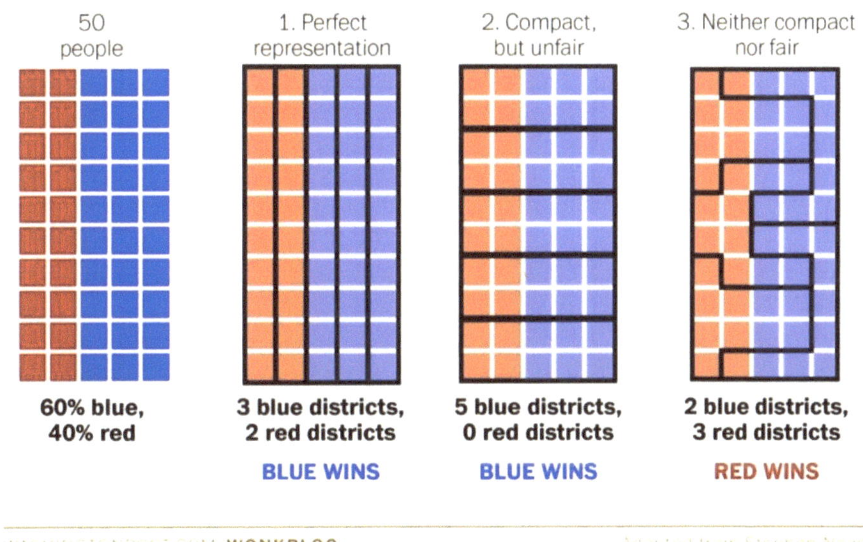

For a most informative (but hilarious) verbal explanation of "gerrymandering," don't miss Stephen Colbert in "The Word—Win, Lose, or Redraw" (see => http://www.cc.com/video-clips/0f673t/the-colbert-report-the-word---win--lose--or-redraw).

"That's the beauty of 'gerrymandering': Instead of the voters getting to pick their leaders, leaders get to pick their voters!"
—Stephen Colbert, *The Colbert Nation* (January 22, 2013)

- -

Why Can't Single-Choice "Preferences" Be Used to Find *The Will of The People*?

So exactly why is it that asking voters for their single-choice preferences cannot be relied upon to find *the Will of The People*—"the collective desire of a group"—whereas Approval Voting can? The problem in a nutshell is that the free world's single-choice, preference-based voting methods merely add up voters' singular preferences to determine the option with the majority of preferences —the preference of the majority. (In the two-option school bus example earlier, this is the polarizing BBQ pork.) But in a democracy, *We the People* **don't care what some arbitrary and ever-shifting 'majority' prefers;** *We* **want to know what's best for** *ALL* **of us—what** *We the* ***COLLECTIVE People* prefer.**

But to understand just what *We the COLLECTIVE People* prefer (i.e. *the Will of The People*), one needs to first understand what a "preference" actually is—how it first relates to an *individual*, and then to *The Collective People*:

pref·er·ence
noun /ˈpref(ə)rəns/
1. A greater liking for one alternative over another or others.

        —http://www.oxforddictionaries.com/us/definition/american_english/preference

The "preference," then, of a single person simply indicates the option that is <u>liked greater</u> than the other options with which it is being compared in a closed set of options. But note that in order to have a "preference," a person must first *evaluate*—put a *'value'* on—all of the options to see which one he <u>values the highest</u> (and thus is liked the greatest). In other words, **the "preference" of a *single person*** (i.e., *the Will of a Person*) simply indicates the option that *the person* <u>values the highest</u>. Using this same logic, then, **the "preference" of a *singular collective people*** (i.e., *the Will of The People*) simply indicates the option that *The Collective People* <u>values the highest</u>.

You've already learned earlier of that *'most peculiar political paradox'* where the preference of a collective society (among three or more options) might not even be ANY individual voter's preference. But here's the precise, logical reason why *the preference of a collective people* (i.e., *the Will of The People*) is NOT represented by the option with the highest total of individual voters' "**preferences**":

As merely the *indicator* of the highest-valued option in a closed set of options, **A "PREFERENCE" HAS NO INHERENT, SPECIFIC, QUANTITATIVE VALUE OF ITS OWN that can ever logically be mathematically aggregated with other preferences into a meaningful total!**

Note that only *known, specific, quantitative values* (e.g., 2 + 3) can be logically aggregated into a meaningful total, and that <u>*unknown and unquantified*</u> values (e.g., $x + y$) *cannot* <u>logically be aggregated into a meaningful total</u>. And thus,

"No 'preference-based' voting methods—comprised of either single-choice, valueless preferences or a *ranked set* of valueless preferences—can ever find *the Will of The People*."

        —Eric Sanders, Director, *The Center for Election Science*,
        December, 2014

How Is It that Only the Value-Based "Rated-Voting" Methods Can Find *The Will of The People?*

What, then, is the best way for a collective society to have its voters evaluate—put a *quantitative value* on—each of its many options so that these quantitative values *can* be summed up to determine which option the collective society values the highest overall (and is thus the "preference" of *The Collective People*—i.e., *the Will of The People*)?

To evaluate (put a *value* on) each option in a closed set of options, a democratic society can ask its members which options they *like*: "**Approval Voting**" (e.g., a vote of approval, a simple 'thumbs up,' clicking an online 'Like,' etc.); or—even better—it can ask its members *how much they like* each option: "**Score Voting**"—just like we numerically *rate* [*score*] products and services, online content, etc. (e.g., from 1 to 5 stars). These <u>quantitative voter *ratings* for each option</u>, all of which express real quantitative values of opinions, can then be mathematically aggregated to see which option is valued the highest overall and is thus most likely to give *The People—as a collective group*—the greatest overall satisfaction.

- -

<u>NOTE</u>: Both Score Voting (aka "Range Voting") and simple, binary Approval Voting are value-based *"rated-voting"* **methods**, where the voter can <u>*rate*</u> (indicate a specific, *quantitative value* for) <u>each and *every* option</u> on the ballot within the specified range of scores. Note that for aggregating Approval Voting, the binary range of specified, numerical scores is considered as either a "0" (disapprove) or a "1" (approve).

- -

In *political* elections, however, the more-highly-nuanced Score Voting requires a somewhat more-expansive ballot to allow each voter to indicate (within a specified range) a 'score'—his personal, quantified rating of 'value' for each option.

Here (below) is a hypothetical example from *The Center for Election Science* of how a filled-in Score Voting ballot and its voter instructions would differ from an Approval Voting ballot:

Score all the candidates below. **The candidate with the most points wins.**
Alexis Sandoval   ⓪①②③**④**⑤
Franklin Hartsdale   ⓪①②③④**⑤**
Daisy Dukes   **⓿**①②③④⑤
David Green   ⓪①②③**④**⑤
Joe Shmoe   ⓪**❶**②③④⑤

- -
Point of Logic #2:
It is important to note that Score Voting (which essentially is *expanded-range*
Approval Voting) is always more expressive for the voter than Approval Voting
because Score Voting *includes* the simple, binary ability of Approval Voting to
fully approve (or not) each and every option.
- -

Nevertheless, it turns out that **simple, binary Approval Voting—*in the political aggregate*—
nearly approaches the results of Score Voting** (see William Poundstone's *Gaming the Vote*,
page 239, for mathematician Warren D. Smith's graph of his computer simulations for various
well-known voting methods in comparison with Approval Voting and Score Voting). But the best
reason to utilize Approval Voting over Score Voting *in political elections* is that Approval Voting
is much easier to understand, quicker to institutionalize, and faster to employ—insofar as Approval
Voting basically utilizes the same ballots, electoral machinery, and procedures that we currently
use for single-choice voting except that *voters are simply allowed to vote for all the candidates
they approve of*, and that *all the multiple-choice approval votes are now counted.*

Understanding all this, you now know why we believe that instituting Approval Voting is the
simplest, most economical, immediate and *precise* common-sense solution for us to find *the Will
of The People*, fix our polarized politics, and create the democracy that *We the People* deserve.

VOTING IN *SANITY*, now,
for finding *the Will of The People*:

**If a collective society wants to find its most highly-rated option, then simply rate
all the options and see which one is the most highly rated.**

After all, why should a collective group select a LESS highly-rated option to act upon? Consider
your group of five friends who want to go to one of thirty movies together: Are you going to tell
them, "Let's NOT pick the movie we collectively rate the highest"?

(DUH!)

*   *   *

Here, then, is our final, best definition for democracy's most important concept—*the Will of
The People*:

the will of the people
phrase
the option, in a closed set of options, that a singular collective people values (rates) the highest.

THE VOTING METHODS OF THE INTERNET AGE

So now that *We* know that only the rated-voting methods (such as Approval Voting and Score Voting) can find *the Will of The People*, you might want to be asking:

Why Is It That No Democracy on Earth Utilizes Any Rated-Voting Methods?

At least four reasons come to mind:

1) Faulty Logic
2) Ignorance (i.e., simple unawareness)
3) Habituated Historical Legislative Procedures
4) Political Conspiracy?

1) <u>Faulty Logic</u>:
Whenever a group of people wants to know what *the group* prefers from a closed set of options, it seems only 'logical' to ask each individual what his or her self-interested *preference* is and then to add up all of these individuals' preferences to see which option is the one that the most people prefer. Unfortunately, this method only finds the option that the most people prefer—*not* the option that *the group* prefers (as you have already proven to yourself in the BBQ Pork vs. Pizza dilemma). And you've even now come to understand that *'a most peculiar political paradox'* resides within all preference-based voting methods: In an election with as few as three candidates comprised of two polarizing demagogues versus everyone's close 2nd choice, it's quite possible that the actual *preference of the <u>collective</u> group* might not even be *ANY* individual voter's preference (and thus may get NO VOTES AT ALL!).

So let's put this *'most peculiar political paradox'*—<u>alternating demagogues vs. everyone's close 2nd choice</u>—into a logical example of simple economics:

> Would you rather have a whole year with a 100% flow (of water, money, great legislation for *you*, etc.) but then a 0% flow the next year, continuing this alternating-pattern indefinitely (just like electing <u>alternating demagogues</u>), or would you rather have a 2nd option of a steady 75% flow, year after year indefinitely? This *2nd* option (let's call it "<u>everyone's close 2nd choice</u>") is, of course, the better option: Besides the simple economics that an average yearly flow of 75% is always better than an average yearly flow of 50% (100% + 0%, divided by 2), the 75% yearly flow is a *steady buildup*, whereas, in the real world of political representation, a polarizing flip-flop of 100% success to 0% failure and back alternatingly tends to elect diametrically-opposed politicians who want to tear down whatever the 'other' party built up.

> ***"We have always known that heedless self interest** [individual self-serving preferences] **was bad morals; we now know that it is bad economics."***
> **—Franklin D. Roosevelt, 2nd Inaugural Address, January, 1937**

2) <u>Ignorance (i.e., simple unawareness)</u>:
Essentially, our earlier social-choice experts never considered 'rated voting' as a legitimate tool for determining collective political preferences, instead thinking that political preferences must first be determined individually and then aggregated to find the option with the highest total of individual preferences (which you now have proven to yourself is a totally-fallacious method for finding

the Will of The People). Even Stanford University economist Dr. Kenneth Arrow's world famous **"Impossibility Theorem"** (as popularized in his 1951 book, *Social Choice and Individual Values*, and which led to his Nobel Prize in economics in 1972) did not consider the *rated-voting methods* as legitimate political voting methods, probably because they had never been utilized in any modern democracy. Instead, Dr. Arrow's "Impossibility Theorem" only evaluated the free world's *existing, preference-based voting methods* and proved that no democracy's *preference-based* voting methods can accurately determine the collective *Will of The People*, noting that **"a clear order of [collective] preferences cannot be determined while adhering to mandatory principles of fair voting procedures."**

—http://www.investopedia.com/terms/a/arrows-impossibility-theorem.asp

- -

> In 1983, New York University Professor of Politics Steven J. Brams, along with Bell Labs' Peter C. Fishburn, wrote a definitive book advocating "Approval Voting" and titled it as such (which was re-issued in 2007). Unfortunately, the wheels of progress seem to turn rather slowly in our de facto two-party 'democracy,' and their sage advice therein has as yet gone unheeded.

- -

3) <u>Habituated Historical Legislative Procedures</u>:

Historically, legislative "voting" on a singular course of action is thought to be a simple process of deciding either *Yes* or *No* on the specific proposal: i.e., *Do we agree with this proposal, or not?* Many hundreds of years ago, secret-ballot voting was often performed by dropping a white ball representing *Yes* or a black ball representing *No* into a ballot box, after which the balls were counted to see which color received the majority of votes. Unfortunately, this voting method really drops the ball (pun intended) by asking voters for just their singular preferences *instead of their quantitative values*, especially since *We* now know that aggregating valueless preferences doesn't work to find *the Will of The People* in the simple, two-option, BBQ Pork vs. Pizza dilemma, and (surprise!) it doesn't even work in a simple *Yes-or-No* decision. Here's why:

> Example: Consider five town selectmen entrusted to making the best collective decision for their town on a simple, singular proposal. Three vote a lukewarm *Yes* but the other two vote an adamant and passionate *NO—NEVER!* (Perhaps they're voting on the school lunch menu whether or not to add some BBQ pork?) Clearly, *the will of the <u>collective</u> group of selectmen* here for the town is the *NO* decision. But in single-choice, preference-based voting, the *Yesses* are the 'majority'—and the minority be damned! Note, however, that when there's only a single option on the ballot to either approve or disapprove, then simple/binary Approval Voting won't work; it needs an *expanded range—Score Voting—* to pinpoint the *overall highest <u>score</u>* for either the *Yes* or the *No* decision by aggregating the *scores* of all the voters for either the *Yes* or the *No* option. (Of course, in local town-board meetings, where proposals for town ordinances are typically discussed first before being voting upon, some of the lukewarm *Yes*-thinking selectmen may be swayed to vote *No* for the sake of the obvious, collective good. But why rely on good-Samaritan selectmen to vote *against* their preferences—or have other selectmen angrily pressure them to do so—when the voting method *itself* [Score Voting] can accurately pinpoint the <u>collective</u> *will of the selectmen*? [e.g., two selectmen's *'No'* scores of "10" each are a higher collective value than three *'Yes'* scores of "6" each])

Do you realize what this means?

THE ENDEMIC ELECTORAL DYSFUNCTION OF OUR SINGLE-CHOICE/ PLURALITY VOTING METHOD IS EVEN WORSE THAN ANYONE SEEMS TO REALIZE: Inescapable <u>common sense</u> tells us that if NO ONE believes in "majority rule" using single-choice voting because it cannot find *the will of the people*—not even in a simple little selection between just two choices!—then aren't all our two-choice *Yes/No, up-or-down* legislative voting procedures for 'majority rule,' as well as our own Supreme Court's *agree/disagree* rulings to find the so-called 'majority opinion,' also *all* just as dysfunctional because they don't find *the collective will* of the voting body but instead select the polarizing 'preference' of just the majority of the members of the voting body?!

- -
CIRCUMVENTING OUR BOGUS
LEGISLATIVE VOTING PROCEDURES

Although the free world's simple *Yes/No* legislative voting procedures are apparently bogus at finding *the collective will of the legislative group*, there's nothing stopping a high-minded group of town selectmen—or any other legislative body—from utilizing Score Voting in a gentlemen's agreement to quickly find their collective body's *most-highly-valued* option and then agreeing to pass it unanimously via the government-mandated voting laws in force. (High-minded readers take note: There's nothing stopping YOU from going to your local town board meeting, quickly proving to the town selectmen via the BBQ Pork versus Pizza example that their single-choice voting methods do NOT find the collective *Will of The People*—not even in a simple *Yes/No* decision to find *the <u>collective</u> will of the Selectmen* [Please feel free to print out and give them our *BBQ Pork versus Pizza* example as well as our *Town Selectmen* example to peruse], and then explaining how they—the town's trustees of smart decision-making—can utilize Score Voting in all of the town's voting procedures and then simply make a gentlemen's agreement to unanimously pass the highest-scored, most-highly-rated option via your state's mandated use of the single-choice voting process.)
- -

4) <u>Political Conspiracy?</u>

How is it that our politicians *and* the media don't seem to want to trace the root cause of our enduring political discontent back to its original source: the arbitrary restriction on voters to indicate just a single-choice preference from among their many options? Is it because our politicians intuitively understand that institutionalizing rated-voting methods will provide a level electoral playing field and thus undermine their two-party duopoly? Is it perhaps also because—as Jon Stewart decried in his closing remarks at his 2010 Washington, D.C., *Rally to Restore Sanity*—our competitive media thrives on controversy and chaos, polarization and conflict to entice greater viewership in order to sell advertising to their commercial sponsors? (In the U.S. presidential primaries of 2016, didn't a master-of-the-media but incredibly polarizing candidate deemed *the most unfavorable presumptive nominee in polling history* capitalize on his ruthless divide-and-conquer strategy using The Media's thirst for sensationalism to catapult himself to the top of the single-choice 'preferences' of the Republican primary voters before going on to win the Presidency by becoming the "most preferred" polarizing candidate of the largest Electoral College faction who was best able to *divide* the country?!)

- -

**The Devastating Effects of
POLARIZATION, CONFLICT, AND WAR**

Back on February 11, 2016, Time.com reported that "The Syrian Center for Policy Research says that 11.5% of Syria's population has been killed or injured" since the war started, while "Some 13.8 million Syrians [out of a total population of 21 million] have lost their means of earning a living. Altogether 45% of the prewar population has been forced to move—including more than four million who have fled the country and 6.36 million displaced within Syria."

—http://time.com/4216896/death-toll-syria-war-470000/

*"If the United Nations means anything, and has any impact whatsoever,
the United Nations and other international organizations have to go in
and at least create a safe zone to let these people come back home."*
—Joe Scarborough, *Morning Joe*/MSNBC, Feb. 11, 2016

<u>Note</u>: The United Nations uses Approval Voting, but only for electing its Secretary-General. Wouldn't it be wise for the United Nations to utilize Approval Voting—or, even better, Score Voting—in *all* its internal voting procedures as well, so that the world's collective of disparate nations can unite around specific, common-ground, common-sense *workable* collective goals towards promoting and keeping a greater World Peace? And what could be better for helping to promote a greater World Peace than instituting worldwide social-choice methodologies—*the rated-voting methods*—that promote common-ground consensus over polarization and conflict?

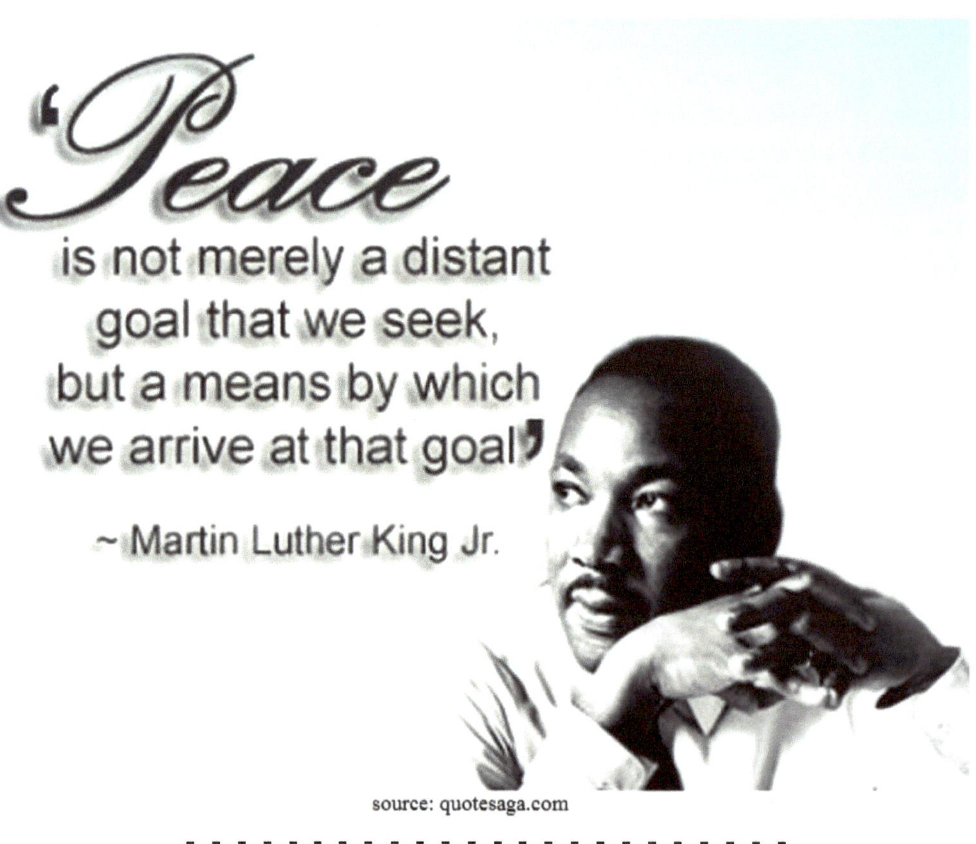

source: quotesaga.com

- -

Who Uses Rated-Voting Methods?

You are undoubtedly familiar with 'approval' methods on social networks such as Facebook (its simple "Like" button), and with 'scoring' methods on commercial websites such as Amazon.com and Yelp.com (1-5 stars) and IMDb.com (the Internet Movie Database, 1-10 stars). Even Twitter (in November, 2015) finally changed its *star* icon representing *favorites* ['preferences'] to a *heart* representing *likes* ['approvals']—thus joining other social media that fully realizes the importance of ratings over preferences. But while these approval- and score-ratings are technically not "voting" methods—because there is no closed electorate making a collective decision, the makers of these platforms understand the efficacy and power of using 'ratings' to promote the most-highly-valued ideas, posts, and products.

But did you know that many other organizations around the world (and not just in technology) also officially utilize Approval Voting and Score Voting to make their collective decisions?

Here is a short list (in small type) of some of the organizations we've found:

Approval Voting:

Intergovernmental
- United Nations - uses approval voting to elect its secretary general

Political Parties
- Colorado Libertarian Party
- Texas Libertarian Party
- Texas Green Party
- Reform Party (US National)
- German Pirate Party
- Modern Whig Party (US National)

Organizations
- Mathematical Association of America (32,000 members)
- American Mathematical Society (30,000 members)
- Institute for Operations Research and Management Sciences (12,000 members)
- American Statistical Association (15,000 members)
- The Webby Awards celebrates achievement found online. They use score voting in their initial round and then approval voting for their final round.

Universities
- Dartmouth College Student Assembly
- San Francisco State University (uses approval voting for faculty electorate, library, and academic senate)
- University of Colorado Student Government (36,000 students, one of the largest student governments in the country)

Score Voting:

Political Parties
- German Pirate Party (North Rhine-Westphalia)
- German Pirate Party (Lower Saxony)

Organizations
- The Harvey Milk Democratic Club, the largest democratic club in San Francisco, uses score voting for their endorsements.

- ESPN.com, uses a score voting procedure to develop rankings for every NBA player from number 500 to number 1.
- Mozilla, the organization that makes the popular Firefox web browser, uses Score Voting to select Mentors for their Mozilla Reps program.
- The Fedora Project, a partnership of free software community members from around the globe, uses Score Voting to select their board members.
- The Central Co-op, an independent, member-owned natural foods cooperative in Seattle, WA, uses Score Voting for their Inside Trustee Elections.
- The San Francisco FrontRunners, a running club, uses Score Voting to select which charity to donate their proceeds to.
- NAVA, the North American Vexillological Association, used Score Voting to identify the best and worst flags on the continent.
- The Webby Awards, celebrates achievement found online. They use score voting in their initial round and then approval voting for their final round.

Entertainment & Sports (Note: some of the winner-selecting rating methods as used by the organizations below are technically not considered "voting" methods)
- American Idol (selecting winners)
- The Voice (selecting winners)
- Dancing with the Stars (selecting winners)
- The Miss America Pageant (selecting finalists)
- Iron Chef (selecting winners)
- Top Chef (selecting winners)
- Cupcake Wars (selecting winners)
- Many Olympic sports, such as gymnastics and figure skating (selecting winners)

Unfortunately, even with the exponential growth of rated-voting methods in the past decade, no *democracy* on Earth currently utilizes any rated-voting methods.

- -

THE SMARTEST POLITICAL PARTY…

After the incredibly polarizing U.S. presidential election of 2016, the smartest political party going forward will henceforth be the first one to specify using simple, multi-choice Approval Voting in all its state primaries to select its *most approved* and thus its *most-generally-electable* candidate for the general election, thereby having a great advantage over all other parties who merely offer just their *most polarizing* candidate via single-choice voting . (Below is a mid-April, 2016 poll showing 'least favorability' in the candidates: highest % = least favorable.)

Of course, the other parties may quickly catch on and adopt Approval Voting as well to level the playing field and find *their* party's most-approved, most generally-electable candidate too. And wouldn't THAT be a good thing for us ALL?

But wouldn't our legislators themselves love to run for office in Approval Voting elections and thus get out from under the yoke of partisan skullduggery—having to kowtow to some private party's agenda they don't fully agree with—and instead become independent, heroic Statesmen who put the needs of the country first (such as enacting some form of government financing for political campaigns so that incumbent candidates running for re-election don't have to waste their own—and *The People*'s—precious time seeking private campaign donations by pandering to wealthy 'sponsors' who expect big 'favors' that aren't in *The People*'s best interests)?

- -

<u>ARRIVING AT COMMON SENSE</u>

Arriving here at this point, then, you too are now something of a voting-methods "expert" because:

1) You fully understand that only the rated-voting methods are capable of finding *the Will of The People*, and that preference-based/single-choice voting methods *cannot* find *the Will of The People* because they erroneously sum up valueless 'preferences.'
2) You realize that we *already* use rating systems (similar to the rated-voting methods of Approval Voting and Score Voting) in our everyday lives to help indicate our highest-rated (and thus our collectively "preferred") products and services, online content, etc.
3) You recognize that there has been an *exponential rise* in the use of rated-voting methods— *"the voting methods of the Internet age"*—by organizations across the world to make their most sensible collective decisions.
4) You have proven to *yourself* that people intuitively utilize multi-choice Approval Voting to find *the Will of The People* in the BBQ Pork vs. Pizza dilemma instead of restricting a bunch of hungry young 'voters' to just a single-choice 'preference,' and you readily understand that your collective of five friends needs to utilize Approval Voting or—better still—Score Voting to find its best, most-highly-rated movie among the 30 from which they can choose.

But clearly, if single-choice voting doesn't even work to find *the Will of The People* in the simplest selection between just two choices as in the BBQ Pork vs. Pizza example, then how could preference-based/single-choice voting ever work in *any* election?! And since Approval Voting is *always* better than single-choice voting (because it *includes* single-choice voting, but not vice versa), then **shouldn't *We the People* utilize simple, multi-choice Approval Voting in *all* our electoral procedures (and Score Voting in all our *Yes/No, up-or-down* legislative procedures) to select our collective society's "most-approved" options (and our legislators' "highest-scored" agreements)—instead of inanely continuing to select the polarizing preferences of arbitrary and ever-shifting 'majorities'?**

> *"We cannot solve our problems with the same thinking we used when we created them."*
>
> **—Albert Einstein**

- -

'APPROVAL VOTING' IN POLLING

Some smart, contemporary polling methods ask, "COULD YOU SEE YOURSELF SUPPORTING…," and "DO YOU FAVOR…," etc. In essence, this is *'Approval Polling'* to indicate the *"favorability ratings"* for candidates in a particular race. (And some polls even utilize *expanded range* Approval Polling—to indicate *how much* each voter favors the candidates over a *range* of feelings, e.g.: from "Strongly approve," "Approve," "Unsure/ No opinion," "Disapprove," to "Strongly disapprove").

Here are a few examples that popped up on TV during the 2016 U.S. presidential primaries that one might have taken cellphone pictures of (and one is even *titled*, "Approval Ratings"):

But, on April 17, 2016, after both the Republican and the Democratic fields had been significantly reduced to show the front-runners of each party, a discussion on *Meet The Press* led by NBC's Political Director, Chuck Todd, essentially brought to light (although it never proffered an answer for) **A MOST INCREDIBLE POLITICAL CONUNDRUM**:

How is it possible that the two "most preferred" front-runners, Donald Trump and Hillary Clinton, are the *"least favorable"* candidates?!

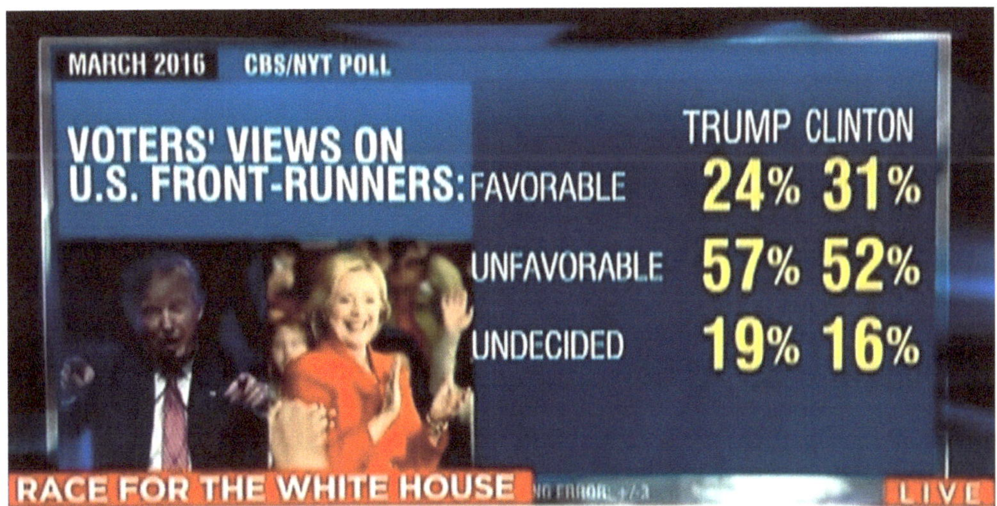

SOURCE: *CNN Newsroom With Poppy Harlow*, 4-3-16

The answer, of course, is that there are two different voting methods being used: Our presidential primaries use **single-choice voting** (same as in our general elections) to indicate the "most preferred" front-runner from each political party, whereas favorability-polling here utilized multi-choice **approval voting** to indicate the *favorability/unfavorability* ratings (i.e., the *approval* ratings) for each of the two front-runners from our entire *collective* society.

And so, shouldn't *We the People* be asking ourselves which voting method do *We* want to utilize for electing the candidate best suited to lead our collective society to peace and prosperity: **single-choice voting**—which selects the "most preferred" candidate of the largest polarizing faction who was best able to *divide* us, or **approval voting**—which elects the "most favorable" candidate of our whole *collective* society who is best able to *unite* us?

At the end of May, 2016, when Hillary Clinton's supporters were claiming that Bernie Sanders should get out of the race because he was spoiling 'front-runner' Hillary Clinton's chances, a wry Facebook posting pointed out the difference between polls for a collectively "most favorable" candidate versus a private political party's "most preferred" candidate:

One might be thinking then, in hindsight, that Hillary Clinton *did* spoil Bernie Sanders' chances of beating Donald Trump. But until Approval Voting or Score Voting is utilized in elections and a slate of candidates actually run to become the most-approved or most-highly-scored candidate under either of these rated-voting methods, then there is no way to accurately claim just who might have been the Approval- or Score-Voting *Will of The People* in the 2016 U.S. presidential race, insofar as expanding single-choice voting into a rated-voting method will not only impact the *kinds* and *numbers* of candidates who run and *how* they will run, but it will also influence *how voters decide to vote* using their new powers to support as many candidates as they like. But when we DO institute Approval Voting, then *We the People* <u>will</u> at least have a "most approved" President who finally *does* have a true mandate of *The People*!

*

<u>Please note</u>: *Voting In Sanity* does not support any particular candidate for office (even though the author has the same last name as one of the 2016 presidential candidates); our sole purpose is to elucidate the best method for *The People* to find their *Will of The People*, mitigate polarization and conflict caused by our dysfunctional voting methods, and give us the democracy *We the People* deserve while at the same time helping to promote a greater World Peace.

- -

There's really nothing complicated about voting in sanity; it's all just common sense, although such common sense still seems to be far too *un*common.

Need some further common-sense convincing for instituting simple Approval Voting?

Imagine if, since the founding of our country, the prescribed voting method has always been simple <u>Approval Voting</u>—where voters approve of as many candidates for an office as they like, and the candidate who receives the most votes wins: There are no political parties or party primaries needed to eliminate 'spoilers,' and a large field of qualified candidates run on their own platforms and owe their allegiance directly to the entire electorate. Multiple, viable, independent candidates all competing on a level political playing field means that big-money donors have little influence (because donations are diluted among the many similar candidates running, and there is less of a guarantee that any specific candidate will win), self-serving lobbyists are less likely to be listened to by politicians who need to get re-elected by <u>all</u> *The People* approving the best candidates from a crowded field, gerrymandering against a large field of independent politicians is unworkable and unheard of, pre-election polls aren't self fulfilling, 'October surprises' don't flip elections to the polar-opposite candidate, and a great multitude of people vote because they have faith in the fairness and efficacy of the electoral process and in the mandate of their elected officials—who are able to pass more broadly-supported legislation quickly and efficiently utilizing simple multi-choice Approval Voting in their internal procedures to put together the most-approved parts of *lots* of bills on the same subject.

But then what if some politician were to come along and say, "OH NO, NO!—we can't allow *You, The People,* to vote for ALL the candidates you might approve of for an office; you have to tell us just your ONE-AND-*ONLY* favorite (even if you like two or more candidates equally), and if he or she doesn't win, then it's just too bad for you— you'll get no input into helping to select anyone from the remaining pack."

WOULD *<u>WE THE PEOPLE</u>* PUT UP WITH THIS FOR AN INSTANT? And, if not, then why are *WE* putting up with it NOW?

*   *   *

Here, then, is our four-word directive for the simple, virtually-no-cost, immediate and *precise* common-sense initiative with which to begin mitigating the dysfunction of our polarizing social-choice methodologies and thus help promote a more peaceful and prosperous planet for us all:

REMOVE THE "OVERVOTE" RULE!
—the rule that discards all such multi-choice votes when a voter selects more candidates/options than the number to which he is arbitrarily being restricted.

This can be done by officially adding just *two words* to our simplest ballot instructions, e.g.: "Vote for one *or more*" (using the same ballots, the same electoral machinery and procedures). **This action thus effectively institutes "APPROVAL VOTING."** And here is a list of its **significant and important benefits:**

- **THE WINNING CANDIDATE HAS THE BROADEST OVERALL SUPPORT** of the electorate instead of merely representing the 'preference' of the largest polarizing faction.
- **NO CANDIDATE IS A SPOILER** to any other, so there's no need for costly and wasteful pre-election primaries that are typically restricted only to registered, pre-polarized partisans and that wind up cutting down the options on the general-election ballot for *the entire electorate*—the largest 'faction' of which includes unaffiliated *non-partisans.*
- **A LEVEL ELECTORAL PLAYING FIELD** means that more candidates will run, and they'll run on their *own* platforms and owe their allegiance directly to *The People* instead of owing their allegiance to just one of two polarizing, self-interested, private political parties whose bosses, platforms, and partisans the candidates needed to pander to in order to become the party's front-runner—beholden to follow the party line to further promote the party's self-serving agenda of taking over full control of the government by "Majority Rule" instead of promoting what *The Collective People* truly want.
- **GREATER POLITICAL COMPETITION** puts an end to "the alternate domination of one faction over another" and the polarized politics and government gridlock that it engenders. And it also means that:
    - campaign 'donations' by private donors, corporations, unions, and lobbyists are diluted and have less negative influence on our general elections and public policy,
    - gerrymandering is ineffective and essentially useless,
    - pre-election polls are no longer self fulfilling in a 'bandwagon' effect (because voters can vote for their longshot favorites *as well as* their approved front-runners),
    - negative campaigning is less effective, elections are less vitriolic, and more voters vote with more faith in their elected officials.
- **INCUMBENTS WILL HAVE TO DO A BETTER JOB** if they want to stay in office.
- **LEGISLATORS WILL BE ABLE TO *DO* A BETTER JOB,** as they utilize Approval Voting to help put together the most-approved parts of *lots* of bills on the same subject and without wasteful pork-barrel projects, quickly facilitating *pre-approved* legislation that best meets the *collective* needs of *The People.*

> *The best governance—just like successful capitalism—requires great competition on <u>a level playing field</u>.*

And if people and politicians want to pinpoint *"the collective desire of a group"* even more precisely among their social choices—and especially whenever they want a *Yes/No* decision on a singular proposal, then they can utilize the best-possible rated-voting method: *expanded-range* Approval Voting—*Score Voting*—to indicate the option that has the highest collective value.

But perhaps *here* is **The Best Reason of All to Institute the Value-Based, *Rated-Voting* Methods**:

Approval Voting (and Score Voting) transforms the way that people actually *think* about collective decision-making, changing the polarizing precept of *It's US against THEM* into a communal spirit that *We're ALL in this TOGETHER*.

And *that* is why the initiative to simply <u>REMOVE THE OVERVOTE RULE</u> and thus institute multi-choice Approval Voting will be the singular, most significant, non-violent and principled action that *We the People* can take worldwide to help find the collective and true *Will of The People* and thus promote a greater World Peace.

- -

On TERRORISM and INJUSTICE:
— *What Are the Causes of Terrorism?* —

When we searched the Internet for *What are the causes of terrorism?* (without quotes), we found that, of the 30,000,000+ Google results, one of them was **"Terrorism: What Are the Major Causes? - Global Terrorism - About.com"** (see => http://terrorism.about.com/od/causes/a/causes_terror.htm).

"There Are Two Causes of Terrorism (by Amy Zalman, Ph.D):
"All terrorist acts are motivated by two things:
- Social and political <u>injustice</u> [underline added]: People choose terrorism when they are trying to right what they perceive to be a social or political or historical wrong—when they have been stripped of their land or rights, or denied these.
- The belief that violence or its threat will be effective, and usher in [political] change. Another way of saying this is: the belief that violent means [efforts] justify the ends. Many terrorists in history said sincerely that they chose violence after long deliberation, because they felt they had no choice.

"This explanation of the causes of terrorism may be difficult to swallow. It sounds too simple, or too theoretical. However, if you look at any group that is widely understood <u>as a terrorist group</u>, you will find these two elements are basic to their story."

And what could be more of an <u>injustice</u> than when the free world's dysfunctional decision-making methods—perpetuated by the entrenched and self-serving powers that be—continue to select polarizing alternatives at the expense of the common-ground consensus?!

Is it any wonder, then, why there are so many <u>frustrated factions</u> around the world ready for a revolution—a peaceful 'political revolution' as Bernie Sanders calls for, or a *violent* revolution as self-serving, megalomaniacal terrorists call for?

"Those who make peaceful revolution impossible will make violent revolution inevitable."
—*John F. Kennedy*

- -

It is well understood that the global war against terrorism is a fight not so much on the battlefield but in the "hearts and minds" of a people—people often polarized by social injustice, and frustrated to the point of thinking they need to turn to violence to effect their just cause (as the American colonists turned to violence to finally break away from the imperious and autocratic English monarchy). But the ability for *The People* to find and implement common-ground consensus over demoralizing polarization—thanks to logical and sane collective social-choice methodologies that accurately find the true *Will of The People*—will likely help mitigate the perceived injustices of conflicted people worldwide and thus help dispel the need for an army of soldiers to force a frustrated 'opposition' into a bitter submission that all too often leads to resentment and hatred over time.

> **"An army of principles will penetrate where an army of soldiers cannot."**
> **—Thomas Paine, "Agrarian Justice," 1797**

*   *   *

Best Definitions for the Four Most Important Concepts in the Free World

Finally, in closing, here are our best definitions for the free world's four most important concepts—"**election**," the "**vote**," "*the Will of The People*," and "**democracy**":

e·lec·tion
noun \i-ˈlek-shən\
the formal process of selecting a person for public office or of accepting or rejecting a political proposition by voting.
> —http://www.britannica.com/EBchecked/topic/182308/election

vote
noun \ˈvōt\
Full Definition of VOTE
1 a: a usually formal expression of opinion or will in response to a proposed decision;
especially: **one given as an indication of approval or disapproval of a proposal, motion, or candidate for office**
b: the total number of such expressions of opinion made known at a single time (as at an election)
> —http://www.merriam-webster.com/dictionary/vote
> —[also] http://law.academic.ru/13497/vote

Note that this broader, more-inclusive definition of "vote" does not define voting as necessarily just choosing a singular preference from among a closed set of options but that it specifically defines "vote" as a "formal expression of opinion" (a rated value), especially as "an indication of [an] approval" (of which the total number of "approvals" may be aggregated in an Approval Voting election to find *the Will of The People*).

"The Vote is precious; it's almost sacred. It's the most powerful, non-violent tool we have in a democratic society."

> —Congressman John Lewis, age 75, who, 50 years earlier, helped lead the *Selma-to-Montgomery March* for voting rights for all people, regardless of color, that turned into *'Bloody Sunday'* (to Jon Stewart, *The Daily Show*, March 9, 2015)

---

the will of the people
phrase
the option, in a closed set of options, that a singular collective people values (rates) the highest

Note that *the Will of The People* is <u>never</u> represented by what a mere 'majority' of people "prefer"!

de·moc·ra·cy
noun \di-ˈmä-krə-sē\
: a form of government in which people vote in elections to directly select their most-highly-valued options or to elect leaders who best represent *the Will of The People*

* * * * * * * * * * * * *

OUR LEGACY

Well, there you have it—*Voting In Sanity*, as promised: not only the 60-second proof that **the entire free world's voting methods are fundamentally incapable of finding the collective *Will of The People*** but also the full knowledge of just *why* this is so—that single-choice voting dysfunctionally selects the preference of the largest polarizing faction instead of finding the collective *Will of The People* as determined by the rated-voting methods of Approval Voting or Score Voting. And you now also understand that the bane of democracy throughout history has been *and continues to be* the inane and arbitrary restriction on voters to indicate just their singular, *valueless preferences* from among their many options—a restriction that only promotes polarization and conflict at the expense of common-ground consensus.

Instituting Approval Voting

Such simple voting-method reform—the institution of Approval Voting—may readily help promote a more peaceful and prosperous planet for us all by finally allowing us to accurately determine the collective *Will of The People*. However, *We the People* are in a bit of a quandary— i.e.: What entrenched, self-serving legislators want to help create a level playing field in electoral politics by instituting Approval Voting and thus significantly reducing their chances of getting re-elected? Nonetheless, if you value harmony over discord, peace and cooperation instead of violent extremism and war, and if you want to help leave as a legacy for your children and loved ones a better world to live in, then *We the People* must not remain indifferent but will have to take action on our own.

> *"Action is the only remedy to indifference—the most insidious danger of all."*
> **—Elie Wiesel, Holocaust survivor (1928–2016);**
> **Nobel Peace Prize recipient, 1986**

And so, just <u>what</u> is the best action for us to take to get rated-voting methods instituted?

But before we lay out our action plan, let's see what went wrong with our own democracy in the presidential election of 2016:

AN UPDATE ON THE EPIC FAILURE OF OUR 2016 U.S. PRESIDENTIAL ELECTION
(How Trump Won the Presidency by Gaming the System)

Now that the 2016 race for the Presidency for the most powerful position in the world is behind us, can anyone legitimately argue that our two "least favorable" candidates—Donald Trump and Hillary Clinton—were the two candidates from which *We the People* should have been voting between for the most important job in the world? With both Donald Trump and Hillary Clinton polling throughout the race together as the "least favorable" pair of front-runners in polling history, it appears that single-choice voting, in the 2016 presidential election, has finally once-again exemplified the most pernicious peril of our dysfunctional two-party system: having to vote for 'the lesser of two evils'—each one in 2016 the "least favorable" candidate of his own political party but somehow, inexplicably, the "most preferred" candidate by the respective partisan primary voters! (And in the case of Donald Trump—*the most <u>unfavorable</u> presidential nominee in polling history,* he won the Republican single-choice primary vote by "the highest vote-count in the history of the Republican Party," as he so often liked to remind us).

So how did the brash and boastful billionaire businessman Donald Trump—with no political or military experience whatsoever (and with little or no experience serving the public's needs)—somehow engineer one of the greatest political upsets in the history of the United States, coming from the "least favorable" candidate in polling history to somehow become the "most preferred" candidate who won the Presidency of the United States?

Here's How It All Went Down

On June 16, 2015, when billionaire real-estate magnate and 'branding' entrepreneur Donald Trump descended from his Trump Tower to take on the press for the Presidency, he shrewdly began the political strategy he would need to propel him into the highest office in the land—the Presidency of the United States—the leader of the free world.

To do this, taking advantage of the dysfunctionality of our bogus single-choice voting method (throughout the primaries and the general election), and complicated by the need to win the Electoral College in the general election, the Trump team carefully crafted a divide-and-conquer political strategy for their reality-TV star, relying upon their candidate's great media skills for 'grabbing' headlines by making the most outrageous, boastful, and politically-incorrect statements—any of which would normally be disqualifying for any 'normal' political candidate.

Trump's initial/official pronouncement speech for the Presidency was so outrageous and politically incorrect that it made New York headlines the next day SCREAM:

But as Donald Trump continued to throw up so many outrageous claims and statements during the campaign, the overwhelmed press was unable to fact-check them all before another one arrived (but isn't this the free press's job—to fact-check the truth of candidates' claims and statements, or is their job simply to just 'report' them all and then let the readers and viewers decide for themselves which statements and claims are simply bogus or bald-faced lies?). Seizing on all the lessons he'd learned over a lifetime of capturing free headlines at any cost *("There's no such thing as bad publicity." –P.T. Barnum?)*, Donald Trump thus branded himself as the bold and brash 'anti-establishment insurgent' who would "drain the swamp" because only "I alone can fix it." Never before had such a media-savvy, unabashed braggart been able to manipulate the media so effectively, and the rapacious press—always hungry for salacious 'news' to beat the competition in the 'news' game—gave Trump so much more coverage than anyone else, that legitimate and well-rounded candidates were unable to effectively get their own positive messages across to the general populace (a serious problem that Jon Stewart had warned us about in his *Rally to Restore Sanity* six years ago). And so, Trump's outgoing tsunami of highly-broadcast boast and bluster quickly helped his campaign take root among a burgeoning pack of faithful followers who were desperate to believe that this 'straight-talking' billionaire was *The People*'s (*their* people's) champion—even though his outrageous, incendiary, and often-contradictory statements and claims by the end of the race would be rated <u>pants-on-fire lies</u> *FAR* beyond any other politician who ran (according to Pulitzer Prize winning <u>Politifact</u>. For the full list of Donald Trump's sixty-plus <u>pants-on-fire</u> prevarications since beginning his race for the presidency, see => http://www.politifact.com/personalities/donald-trump/statements/byruling/pants-fire/).

Donald Trump thus won The Presidency by polarizing the primary- and the general-election electorate to become the singular candidate from the largest polarizing faction who was best able to *divide* us. And it could thus be claimed as well that **Donald Trump won the Presidency by gaming the electoral system**—by strategically becoming the candidate "most preferred" [via single-choice voting] by the majority of voters from the states that held a majority of the electors in the Electoral College. But, of course, this is what ALL the other political candidates would have needed to do in order to win the Presidency! In other words, **OUR BOGUS SINGLE-CHOICE VOTING METHOD 'FORCES' WOULD-BE WINNERS TO USE NEFARIOUS, POLARIZING TACTICS TO WIN THE PREFERENCE OF THE MAJORITY AT THE EXPENSE OF THE COLLECTIVE *WILL OF THE PEOPLE*!**

Here's how the Progression of the 2016 Trump Candidacy looked in *Time*:

Issue of Aug. 22	Issue of Oct. 24	Post-election issue of Dec. 19

Was Trump's campaign strategy of demeaning his opponents by bluster and braggadocio just a carefully calculated plan to present himself as the 'strongman' who could fix all of America's perceived problems, or was Donald Trump (as David Remnick would write post-election in *The New Yorker*, November 28, 2016) just "an ethically challenged real-estate brander who has launched his political career by promoting 'birtherism' [the conspiracy-theory claim that President Obama isn't a natural-born U.S. citizen—thus ineligible to be President], and then run a sexist and bigoted campaign to galvanize his base?" …Or was Mr. Trump's election simply just a matter of dumb luck at having the only other viable 'front-runner' (thanks to single-choice voting) be the uninspiring and fatally-flawed "least favorable" Democrat, Hillary Clinton?

But even as the polls leading up to the election continued to show Hillary Clinton in a strong, significant lead, a couple of the most prominent progressive political pundits and social-commentary comedians continued to liberally sound the alarm that Hillary Clinton was *not* the shoe-in that all the polls were predicting: Academy-Award winning documentary filmmaker Michael Moore quickly produced and released [Oct. 21, 2016] *Michael Moore in TrumpLand* (—essentially, his hour-plus standup performance in Ohio, earlier in the month, as to why the on-the-fence Trump voters or those who were still "undecided" should vote for Hillary Clinton). But the most acerbic diatribe against the Trump candidacy would have to be the one mounted by political-satirist Bill Maher on his HBO *Real Time* show October 14, when he rattled off a list as to why 'undecided' voters should make a decision—and decide NOT to vote for Donald Trump but to vote for Hillary Clinton instead (as he sat alongside ex-candidate Bernie Sanders on his show). Here's the perceptive social-choice prophet, Mr. Maher, speaking directly to his viewers (see => https://www.youtube.com/watch?v=yIMW1C-yy8k), warning us of some not-so-funny dire consequences of authoritarian rule should Donald Trump win, knowing that (as almost always, in single-choice voting) the fate of the American Presidency rests in the hands of The Undecideds: *"I would really like to ask…any 'undecided' voter: As these last fifteen months rolled along, there was no 'breaking point' for ya?—Trump saying he would kill the children of terrorists with drone strikes, physically throwing out 12 million Mexicans, banning all Muslims, giving Saudi Arabia nukes, running a scam university, cheating veterans out of charity money, not paying taxes, picking Putin as his favorite leader, not being able to let go of a feud for a whole week with a beauty queen, the [Trump derogatory] impressions of the handicapped?"*… then, showing a video clip of Trump at a rally in Iowa admonishing the Iowa people for keeping him behind in the polls there: [Trump speaking to the Iowan crowd] *"How stupid are the people of Iowa?"* (Note: Trump went on to win the state of Iowa.)

Nonetheless, even on election day, all the polling was still showing that Hillary Clinton would win the Presidency, perhaps even by a landslide.

Election Eve: WHAT HAPPENED??

On election eve, November 8, 2016, as the dust began to settle, it would turn out that virtually all the professional pundits, prognosticators, and pollsters would get it wrong: The highly-favored Hillary Clinton—generally a 3:1 'overdog'—lost! Donald Trump would go on to win the majority of the electoral-college votes—and thus win the Presidency, while Hillary Clinton would only go on to win nearly three million more of *The People*'s votes—more votes than any losing candidate in the history of the United States! (Note: Many people feel that the Electoral College is an outdated institution from which to pick a President over the popular vote, and we heartily agree. But that's another issue outside of—*and not as important as*—the issue of our nationwide dysfunctional single-choice, general voting-method itself. Nonetheless, it should be fairly noted here that if there were no Electoral College, then Trump and Clinton—and *all* the candidates running—would undoubtedly have been campaigning in a much different fashion.) But even though Donald Trump gave appearances to be the 'highest-energy' candidate in the race (Why sleep when you can Tweet at 3 a.m.?), he won the Presidency in the most despicable manner—by being the most ruthless and most polarizing "most preferred" candidate of the largest faction who was best able to *divide* the country, leaving him to go down in history as one of the least popular incoming Presidents ever!

Think About <u>What *We the People* Are Now Facing!</u>:

Regardless of what you personally thought about either Donald Trump or Hillary Clinton heading into the 2016 U.S. presidential election, thanks to single-choice voting, it has turned out that the greatest polarizing figure of one of our two major political parties—the "most unfavorable" presidential candidate in polling history—has now become the greatest polarizing President of the United States! What could possible go wrong??

Just think: Now that our country has been polarized into two hostile, opposing factions—each one trying to undermine the other, and now that one of the two opposing factions has lost the presidency, virtually half the voters are bitterly disappointed. And now the losing 'minority' party begins its plans anew to undermine the winning 'majority' party…and thus continues our pervasive polarized politics and *The People*'s disgust with 'politics as usual'!

And so, once again, we will never know how unified *We the People* could have been and how quickly we might have been able to address our collective, endemic needs until we utilize a rated-voting method. And when we finally *do* have rated-voting methods for our elections, then all of those polarizing candidates will have to change their tunes if they want to get the most votes from the *entire* electorate (and if they want to even stay in office!). No more pandering to a polarizing majority just to eke out a bare-majority win at the expense of the minority. No more 'politics as usual': *We the People* just aren't going to put up with this nonsense anymore because there'll be so many more good candidates to choose from on the ballot to replace the bad apples. And *We the People* will come to the polls in greater numbers and in greater spirits, knowing full well that we *are* going to be ***Voting In Sanity*** to find *the Will of the People*, fix our polarized politics, and ***Create the Democracy We Deserve!***

But, until then, *We the People* continue to be HOODWINKED by a restrictive single-choice voting method, a method that essentially forces us all too often into choosing our President from between 'the lesser of two evils' from our two-party duopoly—

I cabe to vote.

—as the entrenched incumbents from our two main parties know all too well that *We the People* will have to vote for one of them because *We* don't want a repeat of the year 2000 election where a large number of voters 'wasted' their one-and-only precious vote on some third-party 'spoiler' (Ralph Nader), thus throwing the election to George W. Bush, who should have lost but who would nonetheless go on to become President and, through unwise social-choice decision making of his own, get America involved in the longest-running, most expensive, least productive and most wasteful war that is still ongoing and whose negative effects have thrust the Middle East into a violent turmoil that has cost hundreds of thousands of innocent lives, displaced millions of people (many heading for Europe), and which may ultimately bring down the European Union now that England has 'elected' to leave in its Brexit referendum vote by a narrow "majority rule" (which, as you now know, is a bogus rule in single-choice voting and thus does not indicate the true value as to whether or not the *collective* British people actually value exiting the European Union more highly than not exiting).

*

So why do *We the People* keep allowing bogus voting methods to promote the polarizing preference of the majority over the common-ground preference of the entire collective society? Aren't *We the People* tired of this charade? But what are *We* going to DO about it? It's no good to just stick your head out the window and scream, **"I'M AS MAD AS HELL, AND I'M NOT GOING TO TAKE THIS ANYMORE!"** *We the People* are going to have to DO something about it. And so, maybe we each must ask ourselves, "What can *I* do about it?"

THE PLEDGE

The best action that *We the People* can take to get the systemic electoral change we need, and to fulfill the mandate of ***The People***'s **Declaration of Independence from Irresponsible Representation**, is to make it known throughout the land that *We, as Individuals,* will only favor politicians who publicly support the immediate removal of the overvote rule and thus support the expansion of single-choice voting into multi-choice Approval Voting. And the best way for *US* to make this known is for each of us to take a <u>Pledge</u> to do so.

Ready to promote a greater World Peace by expediting common-ground consensus over polarization and conflict? Think about putting your 'John Hancock' below, and think about getting as many of your friends and family to understand the importance of taking **The Pledge** as well:

The People's Pledge to Remove the Overvote Rule
—thus instituting Approval Voting

I, ____ [name], do Solemnly Pledge to only support politicians who endorse multi-choice Approval Voting—through passing legislation to **Remove the Overvote Rule**—and to <u>*not*</u> support any politicians who refuse to do so!

* * * * * * * * * * * * *

But just how can *We, as Individuals*, specifically use <u>Our Pledge</u> to influence how *We the People* allow ourselves to be governed? Perhaps President Obama explained it best in his final State of the Union Address, January 12, 2016:

[excerpt from the transcript; emphasis added]

" *'We the People.'* Our Constitution begins with those three simple words, words we've come to recognize mean *all* the people, not just some. Words that insist we rise and fall together, that that's how we might perfect our union.

…

"A better politics doesn't mean we have to agree on everything. … Our Founders distributed power between states and branches of government, and *expected* us to argue….

…

"But democracy *does* require basic bonds of trust between its citizens. …

…

Our public life withers when only the most extreme voices get all the attention. …

…

"But that means if we want a better politics—and I'm addressing the American people now—if we want a better politics, it's not enough just to change a congressman or change a senator or even change a president. **We have to change the system to reflect our better selves**.

…

"But I can't do these things on my own. **Changes in our political process—in not just *who* gets elected, but *how* they get elected—that will only happen when the American people *demand* it. <u>It depends on you</u>. That's what's meant by a government *of, by*, and *for* the people.**"

—https://www.whitehouse.gov/the-press-office/2016/01/12/remarks-president-barack-obama-%E2%80%93-prepared-delivery-state-union-address

<u>WHAT *WE THE PEOPLE* CAN DO</u>

Dear Readers,

Want to become part of history? Now is **<u>your chance to influence how *We the People* allow ourselves to be governed!</u>** Insofar as *removing the overvote rule* is a totally peaceful, non-partisan, non-violent action that will help *All the People* (except for our self-serving legislators), then one of the best things that <u>*You the Individual*</u> can do now is to simply write your two state representatives a *letter* (yes, a good-olde-fashioned, personal LETTER that they can actually hold in their little hands!) and explain to them, *in your own words,* that you have just taken a **<u>PLEDGE</u>** never to vote for any candidate/legislator who doesn't support removing your state's "overvote" rule—so that they'll know what *you* now expect of them to ever get your vote again. (You may find your two state representatives here => https://openstates.org/find_your_legislator/). And THEN follow up with a call to ask them if they got your letter, and if—and <u>*when*</u>—they are going to introduce legislation to <u>remove the overvote rule</u>!

When you write your two state representatives (your State Senator and State Assembly Member), and when they finally *do* get the message that their constituents are onto their little self-serving game of getting themselves re-elected at all costs through the single-choice voting method (but at the expense of what *We the People* expect and *deserve*), then they will just have to do the right thing for us (and ultimately the best thing for themselves) and **remove the overvote rule** so that they will forthwith be getting themselves re-elected by *all* of their constituents and have the full <u>mandate</u> and the full <u>*respect*</u> of *The COLLECTIVE Peopl*e of their district (and gain the full return of their own self respect)! And, if you would, go on to explain what this will do for the Legitimacy of our elections in general, for Our Country as a whole (by helping to elect—*through Approval Voting*—a President who would have the full mandate of *The People*), and for a greater World Peace for ourselves and our loved ones—by changing the way that *We the People of Our Planet* actually *think* about "democracy," that ***We're ALL in this TOGETHER*** where *The People—<u>ALL the People</u>*—rule. And **mail a copy of your letter to your local newspaper** as well, so that this most important and popular grassroots initiative for Voting In Sanity by *removing the overvote rule* gains recognition through *The People*'s free press and encourages others who read about it to want to take part too, thus helping to 'pressure' our self-serving legislators into doing the right thing for <u>*We the Taxpayers*</u> who pay their salaries. And if you're savvy with social media, you might want to make up your own posting of your own proud personal participation in the Voting In Sanity initiative to simply remove the overvote rule—the singular, simple and *precise* initiative that can have the greatest impact upon your future and those of the people you love.

…But, if time is short, or you don't feel you can adequately put into words your feelings and frustrations, you might simply mail each of your two state representatives a quick postcard, saying, **"I'm as mad as hell, and I'm not going to take this anymore! If you don't remove the 'overvote' rule, I'm never going to vote for you again!"** (and let them guess why all-of-a-sudden they're getting so many of these angry postcards!!!)

But there's one more thing you can do for yourself and the people you love, and it just could turn out to be the most important thing you may ever do in your life: You now know how to prove that **The Entire Free World's Voting Methods Are Completely Bogus** via the simple BBQ-pork vs. Pizza example; now wouldn't it be great if you could get at least two more people from your friends and family to get on board with *your* Voting In Sanity initiative to <u>REMOVE THE OVERVOTE RULE</u> and get *THEM* to get at least two more of *their* friends and family to get on board to get two more each, etc.—would you be on board with that? And don't forget to post all your proud, ongoing involvement on whatever social media you use, because *We the Voting-In-Sanity People* are *literally* now <u>*ALL in this TOGETHER*</u> to form a 'critical mass'—so to speak— if *We* are ever going to be able to force our legislators into doing the right thing for us in fear that they will never be re-elected to office ever again!!! And definitely <u>send a postcard to your local newspaper</u> to tell them what you have done, and why—as I'm sure that our news-hungry press will want to report on the 'story' of how ***We the People*** **are going to take back our government from our centuries-old, self-serving duopoly by simply refusing to vote for any candidate who refuses to <u>remove the overvote rule</u> once in office!**

And if you're really feeling generous, consider personally gifting a copy of *Voting In Sanity* to some of your civic-minded friends and family—a small investment into a greater World Peace for all the people you love.

IN THE SPIRIT OF THOMAS PAINE'S
COMMON SENSE CONCLUSION:

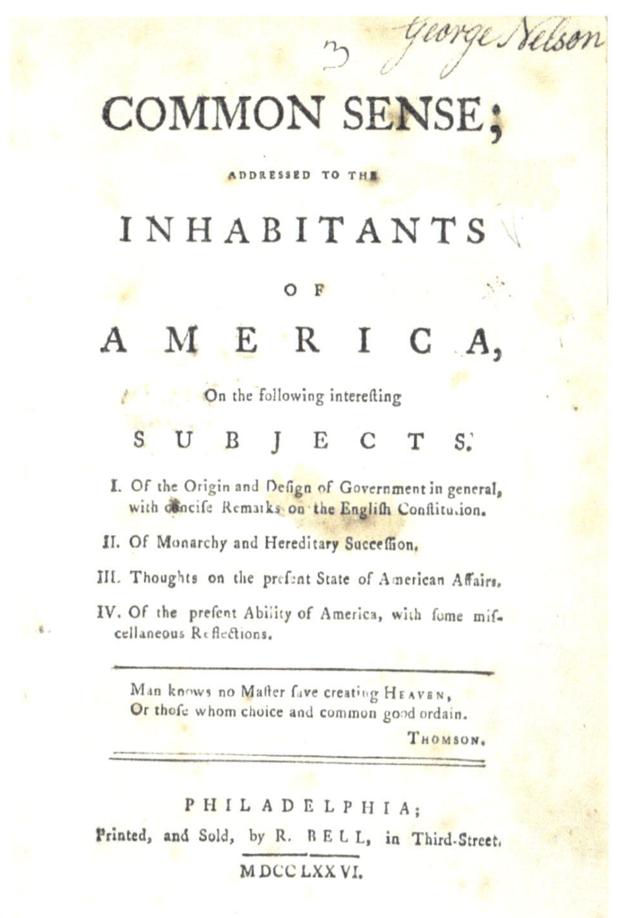

These proceedings may at first seem a bit strange and difficult, but like all other steps to mitigate polarization and conflict that *We* have already passed over, they will, in a little time, become familiar and agreeable. But until *We* fully accomplish Our Goal to <u>Remove the Overvote Rule</u> and thus institute rated voting methods to effect a truly democratic, non-partisan, non-polarizing Democracy, then *We the People* will continue to feel like a person who is putting off some unpleasant business from day to day, yet knows it must be done, hates to set about it, wishes it over, and is continually haunted with the thoughts of its absolute necessity...

...for **Common Sense**
and for
Voting In Sanity...

"...because we know, instinctively, as a people, that if we are to get through the darkness and back into the light, we have to work together."

> **—Jon Stewart; from his inspirational closing remarks, delivered without a teleprompter, at his *Rally to Restore Sanity*, on the National Mall in Washington, D.C., to nearly a quarter million attendees and to a live televised audience estimated at 2.5 million, October 30, 2010**
> (Try => https://www.youtube.com/watch?v=AWX6N-eopOc or => https://www.youtube.com/watch?v=IpUcD9WEC4w)

AN UPDATE ON THE FAILURE OF EGYPT'S NEW 'DEMOCRACY'

In late May of 2012, after the ballots were all counted at the close of Egypt's first free and fair post-Mubarak democratic election, the vote-count showed that none of the thirteen candidates on the ballot received a winning majority (more than half) of the total votes cast, and that a runoff election would have to be held to find a "majority winner" from the top two vote-getters ('top two' in single-choice voting, that is—which you now know is a totally fallacious method for finding *the Will of The People*).

The top-two vote getters (as you might have guessed) turned out to be the two most polarizing candidates at the opposite ends of the political spectrum—the candidates who never spoil each other's chances (while the front-runner, Amr Moussa, whom virtually all the polls had been showing would handily win the election, came in at 5th place).

Outcome: The single-choice voting method was forcing the Egyptian people into two polarized factions—each party trying to undermine the other! (Just like our own polarized politics here in America!)

- -

A Personal Note: On November 1, 2011, your author, George Sanders, tried in vain to warn Egypt, via a personal visit to its New York City Consulate, of impending political polarization and electoral disaster if Egypt used our polarizing 'single choice' voting method in its upcoming election. Unfortunately, the message went unheeded and our worst fears were realized.

- -

The runoff between the top two vote-getters was held in June, 2012. Sadly, no media source at the time (nor to this day) explains just how single-choice voting rewards a pair of polarizing, extremely-dissimilar candidates at the expense of more-centrist candidates—any of whom might have had greater collective support from *The People.*

The Egyptian People had wanted to unite around a peaceful, participatory, representative democracy, but all they would get from their single-choice 'democratic' election was polarization and conflict…and then a complete government takeover by a military strongman:

After the runoff votes were all counted, it is announced that Mohammed Morsi (the religious Muslim Brotherhood candidate) won a close race at 51.7% versus 48.3% for Ahmed Shafik (the secular 'law and order' candidate who was the last prime minister under Mubarak).

Morsi begins to rule as if his electoral "majority win" (via single-choice/runoff voting) has given him the Egyptian People's full mandate (which—as you now know—it clearly didn't), issuing decrees that would essentially give him autocratic rule. Days of local street protests ensue.

As Morsi's leadership proves more and more ineffective and dictatorial, infuriating the military and the secularists, *national* protests start growing.

On July 3rd, 2013, Egypt's Supreme Council of the Armed Forces, led by General al-Sisi, 'removes' [arrests] Morsi, suspends the constitution, shuts down Islamist TV stations, and issues arrest warrants for 300 Muslim Brotherhood officials. Morsi's supporters declare al-Sisi's actions an illegal "military coup."

Large rallies across Egypt hold General al-Sisi in high regard and support the military's removal of the highly unpopular Morsi government, while smaller Islamist rallies mount to protest Morsi's removal. Many people clamor for General al-Sisi to run for the presidency, but Al-Sisi insists he has no interest in politics.

Nonetheless, General al-Sisi finally declares that he has "no alternative but to meet the wishes of the Egyptian people for him to run" (in the presidential election), and on March 26, 2014, announces he will run for the presidency.

The presidential election takes place between the 26th and 28th of May, 2014, and is held without the Muslim Brotherhood's banned Freedom & Justice Party. General al-Sisi wins the Presidency at 97 percent of the votes against his only rival on the ballot. As time goes by, he consolidates autocratic rule by violently cracking down on dissidents and opposition just as his military predecessor Mubarak had done….

And so it seems that the secular dissidents and intellectuals who had wanted to overthrow the military dictatorship of Hosni Mubarak and give Egypt its first opportunity to embrace the blessings of "liberal democracy" only wound up with the return of a harsh military autocracy that they so desperately had wanted to break out from under (and many, if not most, even wound up in jail)!...

*

…which brings us back to George Washington's prophetic forewarning of the potential for such military takeovers of democracies when he wrote to us in his "Farewell Address"—that same paragraph wherein he warned us against "the alternate domination of one faction over another" [paragraph 22, below, in full; **bold** added]. And thus doesn't this also pose a warning for *any* democracy—*including ours*—that continues to use the totally dysfunctional, single-choice/ preference-based voting methods?

> "The alternate domination of one faction over another, sharpened by the spirit of revenge, natural to party dissension, which in different ages and countries has perpetrated the most horrid enormities, is itself a frightful despotism. **But this leads at length to a more formal and permanent despotism. The disorders and miseries which result gradually incline the minds of men to seek security and repose in the absolute power of an individual; and sooner or later the chief of some prevailing faction, more able or more fortunate than his competitors, turns this disposition to the purposes of his own elevation, on the ruins of public liberty.**"

*   *   *   *   *

***Could there be anything more important to human civilization
than the way in which <u>We the People</u> allow ourselves to be governed?***

<u>A PERSONAL NOTE</u> (from Professor Noam Chomsky):

In late August of 2013, when countless millions of Egyptians were protesting the machinations of their new 'majoritarian' President Mohamed Morsi (who was trying to consolidate power as if he had a majority mandate of the collective Egyptian people—which, in reality, he clearly did not), we asked world famous Professor Noam Chomsky what he thought of Approval Voting as "A simple World Peace initiative that could start in Egypt."

…and here, simply, is his mournful reply:

> From: Noam Chomsky [mailto:chomsky@MIT.EDU]
> Sent: Thursday, August 22, 2013 5:42 PM
> To: George Sanders
> Subject: RE: A simple World Peace initiative that could start in Egypt
>
> **I'm afraid the problems, for Egypt and elsewhere, are too deep for technical fixes**

In effect, Dr. Chomsky may have been decrying:

> *"Never can true reconcilement grow where wounds of deadly hate have pierced so deep…"*
>
> **—Thomas Paine, *Common Sense*, 1776 (quoting from John Milton, *Paradise Lost, 1667*)**

*   *   *

Let's not wait for yet another nation and *yet another generation* to be lost around the world to polarization and conflict, and to the violent extremism and civil war it generates. NOW is the TIME for **Voting In Sanity**. Are you IN? If you haven't already done so, go back and

TAKE THE PLEDGE!

… … … … … … … … … … … … …

…and finally, now, onward to some *contemporary* forewarnings about George Washington's fear of "the ruins of public liberty" by "a more formal and permanent despotism":

PROPHETIC FOREWARNINGS
AGAINST A TRUMPED-UP AUTHORITARIAN

"Disrespect invites disrespect; violence incites violence. When The Powerful use their position to bully others, We all lose. … We need the principled [Free] Press to hold Power to account, to call them on the carpet for every outrage—that's why Our Founders enshrined The Press and its Freedoms in Our Constitution."

> —Meryl Streep, acceptance speech for the Lifetime Achievement Award, *Golden Globe Awards*, Jan. 8, 2017 (see => http://www.latimes.com/entertainment/la-et-golden-globes-2017-live-watch-all-of-meryl-streep-s-1483932724-htmlstory.html,)

As you now well know, thanks to our bogus 'single choice' *voting insanity*, Donald Trump—the "most preferred" polarizing candidate of the largest Electoral College faction who was best able to *divide* the country—won the Presidency of the most powerful nation in the world. What could possibly go wrong??

Here's what could possibly go wrong: It could turn out that the self-professed 'strongman' Donald Trump *is* just "a pathological liar" (as his severest critics contend), and that Mr. Trump has no intention, nor the ability, of making America great (again?) nor will he be able to promote America's noble goal towards providing a more stable and peaceful planet for us but is only interested in an authoritarian power-grab (like his authoritarian 'heroes,' perhaps—Putin, Hitler, and Mussolini) to enrich and glorify himself, his family, and his friends—a grab for power to confront a growing list of 'enemies,' particularly the free press that he reviles for <u>factually</u> reporting his own words, especially when he verbally abuses his detractors through personal ad hominem attacks, makes exaggerated or contradictory statements or spouts bald-faced lies, or even when he attacks the free press itself—as when he tweeted less than a month before the election that "The election is absolutely being rigged by the dishonest and distorted media pushing Crooked Hillary – but also at many polling places – SAD."

The Proliferation of 'Fake News'

> "Confusion is an authoritarian tool; life under a strongman means not simply being lied to but being beset by contradiction and uncertainty until the line between truth and falsehood blurs and a kind of exhaustion settles over questions of fact. … An America where we are all entitled to our own facts is a country where the only difference between cruelty and justice is branding."
>
> > —Brian Phillips (*MTV News*, Nov. 16, 2016), "Facebook's Fake-News Problem and the Rise of the Postmodern Right" (see the full article at => http://www.mtv.com/news/2955021/shirtless-trump-saves-drowning-kitten/)

It's no secret that Donald Trump's candidacy was helped immensely at the close of the race by the proliferation of 'fake news' (mostly against Hillary Clinton)—as Trump and his cohorts fanned the flames of fake news by re-tweeting outrageously-unbelievable, totally-fabricated 'stories' posted on obscure conspiracy-theory websites—stories often picked up by the well-known, alt-right, news-and-opinion website Breitbart News Network (which was run by Steve Bannon before taking a leave to become Trump's campaign strategist, and who is now Trump's appointee for White House Senior Counselor). Thousands and thousands of Trump Twitter followers then posted and re-posted these 'stories' on their social media—thus spreading the fake news far and wide, which threw further doubt on the trustworthiness of Trump's only viable opponent (Clinton) but which has now damaged the public's general trust in the News Media itself.

- -

WHAT CONSTITUTES "REAL" NEWS?

When a candidate for the United States Presidency (Donald Trump) claims that *"I could stand in the middle of Fifth Avenue, shoot somebody, and I wouldn't lose any voters"* [Jan 23, 2016], then <u>that</u> constitutes real news (because his proclamation is a fact, and the unusual boast plus its impact on potential voters in a presidential election is a newsworthy story). But when an obviously preposterous conspiracy-theory speculation starts on alt-right chat rooms—that Hillary Clinton and her campaign chairman John Podesta are running a child-sex ring in the basement of some Washington, D.C. pizza shoppe (https://t.co/O0bVJT3QDr, and tweeted out as #Pizzagate)—and gets posted on diminutive conspiracy-theory/white-supremacist websites and then gets picked up by high-ranking Trump supporters to get tweeted out as a possible 'fact' that should be investigated until *"U decide"* (according to a Nov. 3, 2016 tweet by retired General Michael Flynn—whom President-elect Trump subsequently tapped for his National Security Advisor), then the only real "news" here is how so many folks could be so delusional to believe such Fake News—a totally ridiculous story that inspired one delusional man post election to drive from North Carolina with an assault rifle to shoot up the pizza shoppe itself (no one hurt—*this* time), explaining to authorities afterwards that he was there to "self investigate" the story.

- -

As Political Hijinks Reign Near the Close of the Election…

All throughout the race, Donald Trump was able to pin "Crooked Hillary" to a 'scandal' that, when she was Secretary of State, she used a *private* email server for her State Department emails that may have contained highly classified documents on it, after she removed over 30,000 'personal' emails from it before turning her emails over to the FBI for scrutiny—a case closed by FBI director James Comey on July 5, 2016, but not before holding an "unprecedented" news conference, publicly calling Clinton "extremely careless" but withholding recommendation for prosecution.

On July 23, 2016, WikiLeaks released 20,000 hacked emails from the Democratic National Committee—emails that showed a systematic bias against Bernie Sanders by the DNC leadership, causing DNC chairwoman Debbie Wasserman Schultz to resign just before the Democratic National Convention. (And further WikiLeaks of hacked Democratic Party emails showed that the DNC interim chair replacement, Donna Brazile, had given primary-debate questions to Hillary's campaign to help Clinton at the expense of Bernie Sanders.)

On July 27, 2016, Donald Trump, at a news conference, seemed to publicly invite Russia to hack into Hillary Clinton's emails (see => https://www.youtube.com/watch?v=3kxG8uJUsWU): *"Russia: If you're listening, I hope you're able to find the 30,000 emails that are missing."* (Note: By December 9, 2016 [post election and ongoing], "all seventeen U.S. intelligence agencies"—

including the CIA and FBI—have now concluded with "high confidence" that Russia, likely under the direction of Putin, provided WikiLeaks with the Democrats' hacked emails for the purpose of helping Donald Trump win the presidency, while Republican Party emails, also likely hacked by Russia, were never publicly released. See => http://www.nytimes.com/2016/12/09/us/obama-russia-election-hack.html?_r=1)

…a Pair of 'October-Surprise' BOMBSHELLS!:

But, as the continuous drip-drip-drip of the WikiLeaks hacked Democratic-party emails slowly undermined the Clinton campaign, Secretary Clinton finally got a break from all the political bad news: On October 7, just a month before the election, the Washington Post released a 2005 video clip, that it had just obtained, of reality-TV-star Trump speaking lewdly 'off-mic' to television-host Billy Bush about women Trump might meet and typically wouldn't be able to stop himself from kissing and fondling, saying, *"I don't even wait. And when you're a star, they let you do it, you can do anything … grab them by the pussy—you can do anything"* (see => https://www.washingtonpost.com/politics/trump-recorded-having-extremely-lewd-conversation-about-women-in-2005/2016/10/07/3b9ce776-8cb4-11e6-bf8a-3d26847eeed4_story.html?utm_term=.5c6c440c3a27).

Although this story of Trump's admitted penchant for sexual assault would slowly peter out (in the weeks ahead), it was less than an hour after Trump's lewd remarks were first publicly exposed that WikiLeaks started releasing a trove of Democratic hacked emails, this time from John Podesta's email account (see => http://www.politifact.com/truth-o-meter/statements/2016/dec/18/john-podesta/its-true-wikileaks-dumped-podesta-emails-hour-afte/).

But the worst news of all for Hillary Clinton's campaign may have been when FBI director James Comey publicly notified Congress on October 28—*just eleven days before the election*—that he was reopening the inquiry into Clinton's private emails that he'd closed back in July (see => http://www.nytimes.com/interactive/2016/10/28/us/politics/fbi-letter.html?_r=1), only to make headlines against Clinton again *just two days before the election* when he proclaimed that nothing had been found.

- -

IMPORTANT NOTE: October-surprise Bombshells that try to flip elections only work when there are just two diametrically opposed parties—each party trying to undermine the other. (But note: **In Approval Voting elections, if the top contender falls from grace,** *We the People* **get the** <u>next</u> **"most approved" candidate!**)

- -

Perhaps this was why Bill Maher, just four days before the election, was warning the viewers on his HBO show in *Real Time* that Hillary Clinton <u>could</u> lose this election, exhorting his liberal/progressive viewers to get out there and VOTE, because, *"This [election] is a slow-moving right-wing coup that we are witnessing. When the FBI is politicized to this degree, working with Russia, hacking one side, this is a coup, and this could fucking happen in this country, so I don't want to hear any bullshit about 'she's [Hillary's] got it in the bag'"* (as reported on Breitbart.com—see => http://www.breitbart.com/video/2016/11/04/maher-slow-moving-right-wing-coup-in-us-i-dont-trust-nc-gop-not-to-hack-voting-machines/). Of course, we all know how the election turned out: Donald Trump *did* get more votes than Hillary Clinton, although only in the states that counted most.

Two Pre-election Admonitions Against a Trumped-up Authoritarian:

Donald J. Trump had boasted all throughout his campaign, "I know how to win." And so he did—strategically speaking. But at what cost to civility, to the dignity of our democracy, and to the way that we are perceived around the world? The way in which Donald Trump won the Presidency has sometimes been compared to the way in which Adolf Hitler aroused a crowd and used polarizing tactics to build up a following and endear himself to the largest faction of a fractured electorate. And as the political pundits (including Hillary Clinton) throughout the race compared Donald Trump's bombastic behavior to some of the most demeaning and dangerous authoritarian figures in history, Hitler included, an astute assistant history professor, on March 11, 2016—<u>a full four months before Trump's nomination</u>—published an article in Salon.com that proved especially insightful as a cautionary warning to the American People about the dangers of a trumped-up authoritarian 'savior' if Donald Trump were somehow able to win the Presidency and then consolidate presidential powers to become an authoritarian despot who uses the government to reward himself and his friends at the expense of all others while vanquishing the growing 'enemies' on his list—especially the free press that Mr. Trump was constantly accusing of trying to rig the election against him.

– excerpts from the Salon article of March 11, 2016 –
by Bellarmine University assistant professor Fedja Buric
(four months before the nomination of Donald Trump)
"Trump's not Hitler, he's Mussolini: How GOP anti-intellectualism created a modern fascist movement in America"
http://www.salon.com/2016/03/11/trumps_not_hitler_hes_mussolini_how_gop_anti_intellectualism_created_a_modern_fascist_movement_in_america/

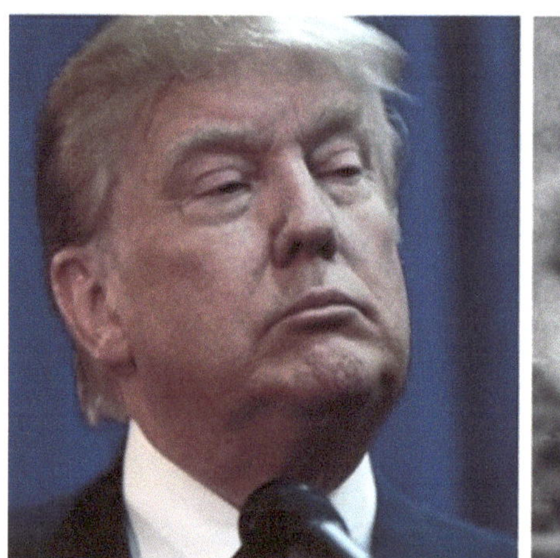

[composite pictures added]

Like Mussolini, Trump rails against intruders (Mexicans) and enemies (Muslims), mocks those perceived as weak, encourages a violent reckoning with those his followers perceive as the enemy within (the roughing up of protesters at his rallies), flouts the rules of civil political discourse (the Megyn Kelly menstruation spat), and promises to restore the nation to its greatness not by a series of policies, but by the force of his own personality ("I will be great for" fill in the blank).

"Fascist leaders made no secret of having no program" [quoting esteemed fascism historian Robert Paxton's acclaimed 2004 book, *The Anatomy of Fascism*]. This explains why Trump supporters are not bothered by his ideological malleability and policy contradictions: He was pro-choice before he was pro-life; donated to politicians while now he rails against that practice; married three times and now embraces evangelical Christianity; is the embodiment of capitalism and yet promises to crack down on free trade.

Like Mussolini, Trump is dismissive of democratic institutions. He selfishly guards his image of a self-made outsider who will "dismantle the establishment" in the words of one of his supporters. That this includes cracking down on a free press by toughening libel laws, engaging in the ethnic cleansing of 11 million people ("illegals"), stripping away citizenship of those seen as illegitimate members of the nation (children of the "illegals"), and committing war crimes in the protection of the nation (killing the families of suspected terrorists) only enhances his stature among his supporters. The discrepancy between their love of America and these brutal and undemocratic methods does not bother them one iota. To borrow from [historian] Paxton again: "Fascism was an affair of the gut more than of the brain." For Trump and his supporters, the struggle against "political correctness" in all its forms is more important than the fine print of the Constitution.

The Very Fascist Origins of Trumpism

That white supremacist groups back Donald Trump for President of the United States, and his slowness to disavow the support of David Duke [former Imperial Wizard of the Ku Klux Klan], all illuminate the fascistic origins of Trump the phenomenon. … Like Fascism, Trumpism has come about on the heels of a protracted period of ideological restlessness. Within the Republican Party this restlessness has resulted in a complete de-legitimization of the so-called GOP establishment.

Fascism promised people deliverance from politics. Fascism was not just [a] different type of politics, but *anti-politics*. …

It is therefore no coincidence that the most common explanation Trump supporters muster when asked about their vote is that "He is no politician."

Trump has successfully wedded this anti-Enlightenment mood with the anti-political rage of the Republican base. … Still, for a fascist to be accepted as legitimate he has to move the crowd and from the very beginning of his candidacy Trump has done this by stoking racial animosity and grievances. It is no coincidence that the Trump phenomenon emerges during the tenure of the first black President. It bears remembering that Trump's first flirtation with running for office was nothing more than his insistent, nonsensical, irrational, and blatantly racist demand that President Obama show his birth certificate and his Harvard grades. This was more than a dog whistle to the angry whites that the first black President was not only un-American, literally, but that he was intellectually inferior to them, despite graduating from Harvard Law.

Like Mussolini, Trump is lucky in his timing. … Islamophobic euphoria [is] sweeping rightwing and fascistic movements into power all across Europe.

> But it bears reminding that the [Trump-rally] crowds have transformed Trump as well … Simultaneously, he has gotten more confident on stage, bolder in his outrage proposals (ban all Muslims from the U.S.), and more theatrical.
>
> We should be warned that fascist demagogues are often made on the sly, almost imperceptibly, and that the fires they stir up tend to spread rather quickly.
>
> Once unleashed, the demons of history are too difficult for any individual to resist on his or her own no matter what their backgrounds or political beliefs of the moment. **<u>This is why resistance to such atrocities always requires a movement, a community</u>** [<= bold/underline added] ….
>
> Today, the echoes of Fascism are all too audible to anyone willing to hear them.

Was Professor Buric calling for a worldwide movement to resist authoritarian fascism wherever it may appear? And would YOU want to be part of such an anti-fascist <u>worldwide community</u> of freedom-loving peoples through Voting In Sanity?

Perhaps Republican political strategist Steve Schmidt, on October 18, less than a month before the election, best explained how Donald Trump's presidential race was like a cancer undermining our country [excerpted from https://www.youtube.com/watch?v=AbRh0KZWhaQ, bold added]:

> "He [the President] is the steward of the office first occupied by George Washington. Part of our inheritance is our democratic system. That's what the office of President of the United States is about. And when it's undermined by a candidate for the Presidency, we have to understand how cancerous that is. **Fascism did not rise in the thirties because it was strong but because democracy was weak.** We need to understand that."
> —Steve Schmidt, Republican strategist and political analyst,
to Brian Williams, October 18, 2016

Donald Trump certainly did run the most polarizing and vitriolic race to win the Presidency. But was this all just a ruse to strategically win, so that he could go on to do some really great things for the America he professes to love? (One might then ask: Has Donald Trump *ever* done great things for the America he professes to love?) Or is this all just a self-serving power-grab for himself to become a fascist authoritarian on the ruins of public liberty? Or perhaps something in the middle? Or maybe the office of the Presidency will change him as history or tradition teaches us (or as Obama hopes)? Only time will tell. But certainly *We the American People* need to protect our centuries-old, hard-fought democracy against *any* such authoritarian figure who would consolidate his personal power at the expense of *The People's Liberty*, insofar as the lessons of history have always shown us that "power tends to corrupt, and absolute power corrupts absolutely."

In any event, when our 2016 election for the U.S. Presidency concluded with a Trump victory in the wee hours of the morning on election eve, Donald Trump's teleprompted victory speech quickly proclaimed, *"To all Republicans and Democrats and independents across this nation, I say it is time for us to come together as one united people,"* and that *"I pledge to every citizen of our land that I will be President for all Americans, and this is so important to me."* But there just may be some trepidation by the broad swath of Americans that Mr. Trump savaged, mocked, and demeaned along the way to his carefully-crafted Electoral College victory, that somehow this most boastful braggart and proven prevaricator would now turn out to be the *collective* People's champion instead of merely the champion of his own self interests.

And so *We as Individuals* must ask ourselves: Are *We the People* best off with our "most preferred" new leader, Donald Trump, to make America great (again)—even though he has personal business ties with other authoritarian nations and billionaire business leaders around the world and who now has incredible conflicts of interest with his own office of The Presidency (undiminished by his claim that his businesses will be run by his children without him)? Or do <u>you</u> think it likely that *We the People* (and the whole World of People who look to us for inspiration and leadership in the global fight for liberty and justice for all) would be better served if our voting method had enabled us to elect our most favorable, "most approved," *most-highly-valued* candidate who was best able to collectively *unite* us toward a greater world of peace and prosperity for *all*, instead of selecting the singular candidate who was simply the "most preferred" because he was best able to polarize and *divide* us?

What *We the People* Need to Do to Protect Our Nation's Liberty

When Trump and his cohorts' tweets and re-tweets help fuel a fire of 'fake news' to obfuscate Truth itself, allowing the potential for an authoritarian despot to gain the power of The Presidency and rule at his whim by being able to define **Truth** to his own liking, and especially if he is able to weaken or cower our Constitutional First Amendment Rights to **<u>freedom of the press</u>** to responsibly report true **Facts**, then *We the People* need a responsible free press now more than ever! But, above all, *We the People* truly must take action *now* to protect our hard-fought Freedom, because:

> ***"To abandon facts is to abandon freedom. If nothing is true, then no one can criticize power, because there is no basis upon which to do so. If nothing is true, then all is spectacle. The biggest wallet pays for the most blinding lights."***
> —Timothy Snyder, the Housum Professor of History at Yale University and author of *Black Earth: The Holocaust as History and Warning* (from his Facebook posting of Nov. 15, 2016, his insightful and poignant 20-point guide to defending democracy against authoritarianism => http://qz.com/846940/a-yale-history-professors-20-point-guide-to-defending-democracy-under-a-trump-presidency/)

As a matter of <u>fact</u> (literally), here is President-elect Trump's end-of-the-year tweet to us all, his final greeting, gloating—perhaps the fitting 'tribute' to the epic failure of our 2016 presidential election:

Happy New Year to all, including to my many enemies and those who have fought me and lost so badly they just don't know what to do. Love!

8:17 AM - 31 Dec 2016

Isn't it ironic now, in the aftermath of the election, as we have seen a spike in hate crimes across the country, that the man who stoked the flames of racism and xenophobia is now being called upon to put the fire out? But if the crowds of thousands upon thousands of angry protestors roaming the city streets following Donald Trump's election is any indication of the future, then *We the People*—the *collective* electorate that prefers the "most highly-rated" candidate who *unites* us over the candidate "most preferred" by just the largest polarizing faction who was best able to *divide* us—need to protect Our Liberty by joining together in the most important but non-violent grassroots 'political revolution' of our lifetime: INSTITUTE THE RATED-VOTING METHODS—APPROVAL VOTING and SCORE VOTING, so that Our Leaders will have a mandate from our whole, *collective* society! But until *We the People* DO get our act together (Did you think about signing <u>The Pledge</u> yet?), then *We the People* will continue to be hoodwinked by the polarizing forces of a de facto two-party duopoly, as we sit around and watch our self-serving and most-polarizing candidates in their private political parties take full advantage of the ignorance of the American electorate and its dysfunctional single-choice voting method. IF EVER THERE WAS A TIME THAT *WE THE PEOPLE* NEED TO <u>REMOVE THE OVERVOTE RULE</u> TO BEGIN INSTITUTING THE RATED-VOTING METHODS, *NOW* IS THE TIME!!!!!—But, until then, folks, fasten your seat belts, as we just may be in for a long and bumpy ride!

<u>Author's Note</u>

We, the Authors, herein claim to have no direct link to politicians of any political affiliation, nor to be influenced by any remunerations (bribes, payoffs, 'donations,' etc.), nor by any specific persons or parties other than ourselves.

We, the Authors, thus do solemnly Pledge to do our best to herewith hold all politicians to their moral responsibilities to effect what they were elected by *The People* to do—to find the best consensual solutions to Our most important and endemic Problems. And we hope that you, too, take up this Pledge along with us.

Now that you have come to realize that the simplest form of value-based rated voting—*Approval Voting*—is an intuitive process that promotes a collective peace and prosperity instead of a divisive majoritarian rule by the 'most-preferred' polarizing faction, then you must also realize that the implementation of the common-ground consensus for *the Will of The People* via the utilization of Approval Voting and Score Voting in Our Electoral and Legislative Procedures, as well as in our Judiciary, will assuredly come to fruition sooner or later, and thus our entrenched politicians would be wise to get on board with "a good idea whose time has come" as soon as possible before *We the People* move on to better choices!

- -

George Sanders

January 20, 2017

What if they gave a war
and nobody came.....

If you are finally fed up with polarized politics, and the divide-and-conquer strategy of tribalism and racism that *It's US Against THEM* (whoever "them" keeps turning out to be all over the globe), then how would you like to join the greatest *tribe* in the world, <u>*We the Collective People of Our Planet*</u>, and the greatest *race* of all, <u>*the human race*</u>, because, in this ever-more-complex and inter-dependent world, *We the Collective People of Our Planet* are really **ALL in This TOGETHER**, so we might as well utilize our best social-choice methodologies to figure out what's collectively best for *all* of us and put an end to our petty rivalries that only wind up seriously hurting ourselves, our families, and our loved ones over the long run.

JOIN US

in our not-for-profit, free, global humanitarian initiative for a greater WORLD PEACE

Sign

<u>**THE PLEDGE!**</u>

…and send a copy to each of <u>your two state representatives</u> (you can find them here => https://openstates.org/find_your_legislator/) …

…and CALL THEM shortly thereafter and PERSONALLY ASK THEM if they are going to PROMOTE LEGISLATION TO REMOVE THE OVERVOTE RULE and <u>WHEN</u> are they going to do it?!

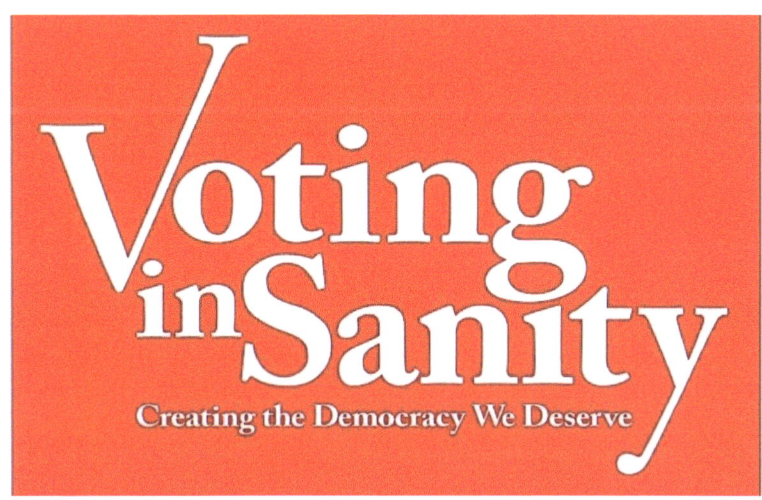

Are you IN?